KU-769-224

Contents

SIMPLY A GREAT MANAGER

THE FUNDAMENTALS OF
BEING A SUCCESSFUL MANAGER

Michael Hoyle & Peter Newman

Copyright © 2011 Michael Hoyle & Peter Newman
Cover design: Jim Banting

Published in 2011 by Marshall Cavendish Business
An imprint of Marshall Cavendish International

PO Box 65829, London EC1P 1NY, United Kingdom
info@marshallcavendish.co.uk

and

1 New Industrial Road, Singapore 536196
genrefsales@sg.marshallcavendish.com
www.marshallcavendish.com/genref

Other Marshall Cavendish offices: Marshall Cavendish Corporation. 99 White Plains
Road, Tarrytown NY 10591-9001, USA • Marshall Cavendish International (Thailand)
Co Ltd. 253 Asoke, 12th Flr, Sukhumvit 21 Road, Klongtoey Nua, Wattana, Bangkok
10110, Thailand • Marshall Cavendish (Malaysia) Sdn Bhd. Times Subang, Lot 46,
Subang Hi-Tech Industrial Park, Batu Tiga, 40000 Shah Alam, Selangor Darul Ehsan,
Malaysia

Marshall Cavendish is a trademark of Times Publishing Limited

The right of Michael Hoyle and Peter Newman to be identified as the authors of this
work has been asserted by them in accordance with the Copyright, Designs and Patents
Act 1988.

A CIP record for this book is available from the British Library

ISBN 978-981-4351-09-6

Printed in Singapore by Fabulous Printers Pte Ltd

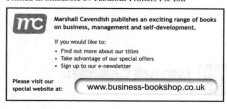

Warning to Readers

Many readers may expect this book to contain a host of sophisticated ideas about personal relations, psychology, information technology and so on. It doesn't.

Some readers may expect the ideas we present to be complicated, difficult to understand or new. They are none of these things. In fact, this a simple book written in a simple style using simple concepts.

This is not an apology. It is not that we are treating you, our readers, as though you had limited intelligence. It is just that *managing is simple* and we have found no reason to make our explanations anything other than simple.

Preface

We have written this book because when we ran a workshop on managing organisations at a strategic level, we were accused of making it all too simple: "There was nothing sophisticated or complex in your presentations." Our immediate response was to say, "That's the whole point, managing *is* simple, but – to add the words of one of the world's leading management gurus – it isn't easy."

This led us to ask ourselves what *is* it that on the one hand is simple, but on the other is not easy to do properly? We can say that arithmetic is simple because you can use your fingers, but it isn't easy until you have learnt to count and recognise the meaning of numbers. What, we asked ourselves, is the analogous answer for *managing?*

With the help of the library at the Chartered Management Institute, we searched the literature for existing principles for managing. Recent management books that mentioned the word "principles" mostly told readers how to do certain things in certain situations. However, they tended to lack real principles that aspiring managers could use in guiding their managerial life.

So we set out to identify a number of basic principles (we like to call them "virtues for managing") that are exhibited by successful managers, and that need to be followed by all of us when we have something or somebody to manage. Our "virtues" are derived and distilled from real managers' experience. Each of them is very simple and straightforward, as might be expected of something that has stood the test of time. We believe that they can be used in managing an organisation, an individual, or indeed anything and everything.

We have tried to make the book as readable as possible for everyone. We see our readers as people who want to be good managers and are seeking to improve their level of performance. We hope that the time you invest in reading the book, in thinking about its contents and, more importantly, in following our principles in everyday practice, will be well rewarded.

We owe a great deal to a great many people from whom we have learnt so much: our teachers and professors, our colleagues and bosses, our clients, our friends and our families. Without them this book would not have been conceived or written. We sincerely thank them all.

We are grateful for the comments of those who read earlier drafts of the book: Dermot Bates, Gordon Gullan, David Hoyle, Jon Richings, Paul Smitheram and Philip Tasch, as well as final-year graduate business students at the University of Surrey, who gave us the benefit of their experience as international managers and as potential readers.

We are indebted too to our illustrator Ray Jelliffe and to everyone at our publisher, Cyan Books, especially Martin Liu. Their contributions have been invaluable.

Finally, we cannot end without thanking our wives, Marion and Lynda, for their love and support not only throughout the preparation of this book, but also when we have been away from home working as managers and consultants.

MHH AND PGN
UPTON GREY AND FARNHAM
SPRING 2008

01

Managers and Managing

Who are Managers?

Many people think of managers as people who are special, who have particular talents, who are well paid, and who are in charge of something important. No doubt there are many managers that fit this description. But equally, there are millions of other people who go about their daily life being a manager but without thinking that what they do is anything special. Many of them are not called managers, or even recognised as doing the job of a manager.

Our dictionary defines a manager as "a person conducting a business, institution, etc," but we think it is more realistic and useful to use the following definition:

 A manager is the person responsible for a group of people or things or activities.

This includes the mother responsible for her children, the priest responsible for parishioners and the teacher responsible for pupils, as well as the sales manager responsible for sales staff. It includes the accountant responsible for an audit, the politician responsible for a ministry, and even the little girl asked to hold her younger brother's hand when they cross the road. It includes the individual responsible for the office building, the factory, the fleet of vehicles, and the training of staff, as well as the intangible goods such as intellectual property and relationships of all kinds.

Being a manager is not a modern role that depends on computers or degrees or technology. Imagine what it took to build the Great Pyramids at Giza and you have to admit that the ancient Egyptians must have had successful managers. The role has probably existed since time immemorial – perhaps since Adam was charged with looking after the Garden of Eden.

What is Managing?

Of the many definitions of managing, we prefer the following:

 Managing is the process by which the manager discharges his or her responsibilities.

For example: how does the chairman of a company secure the long-term survival of the business? How does a mother respond to her small daughter when she comes home from school in tears, saying that her teacher is horrible and she won't go to school tomorrow? In both cases, they have to decide what to do. It may be after careful deliberation, or it may be an intuitive response that reflects what they *usually* do, or what they have been *trained* to do, or what their character and personality *tell* them to do.

Sometimes these decision-making processes (or managing) lead to good outcomes, sometimes not. The surprising thing is that nowhere in our education are we taught the principles of managing that we should follow. This is unusual, for as we grow and mature we encounter many key principles that we learn to follow in our everyday lives, or that operate in specialist areas in the wider world. For example:

- In bringing up children, we are told about the importance of bonding with babies, the need to show them affection, to talk to them, and so on.
- The law operates according to certain principles: that a suspect is innocent until proven guilty, that hearsay evidence is unreliable, that witnesses must not be coerced.
- In warfare, codes of conduct are in operation: civilians should not be attacked deliberately, responses to aggression must be proportionate, and the dignity of prisoners of war should be respected.
- In ball games, children learn to keep their eye on the ball and watch their opponents.
- In accounting, it is important to differentiate between cash items and non-cash items, between assets and liabilities and so on.
- In the medical field, there are principles of behaviour beginning with the Hippocratic Oath.

Principles of Managing Successfully

Is there a set of principles of managing that can be followed to allow ordinary people to be great managers? We believe that there is. Why? Because of what we have observed during 40 years of managerial experience.

First, ask yourself who is the best manager you have ever known. When we asked ourselves this question, we didn't say that Julia was the best financial manager, or that Tom was the best cricket manager, or that David was the best project manager, or that Andrew was the best manager of a legal practice, or that Sarah was the best hospital manager. No, we said that Julia or Tom or whoever was the best *manager* we have known – in other words, what they managed was irrelevant; it was how they did it that was noteworthy.

Second, do you believe that good managers do basically the same thing albeit in different circumstances, or do you think that they all do something different? When we asked ourselves this question, we thought that they probably were doing the same (or very similar) things, although we weren't sure quite what it was that they had in common. In fact, when you put this conclusion together with the thought that the manager has been around since about the time of Adam and Eve, it seems plausible that there is just one set of principles for all good managers to follow.

This book is about those principles. In other words, it is about how to be a great manager. It is about how to apply these principles no matter what circumstances you, the manager, find yourself in: whether you are thinking about discharging your responsibilities over the next hour, the next day, the next week, the next month, the next few years or whatever. For example:

- What do you do when your boss gives you yet another job to do, but you have promised your spouse that you will be home on time tonight – and it is your wedding anniversary?
- What do you do when your best member of staff suddenly resigns?
- Or when you are told that you have to reduce the number of your employees by 20% within a week?
- Or when ...

Are there guidelines or principles to help you, the manager, cope with these situations? Or are you going to worry, panic and act instinctively without the slightest idea whether your actions will make things better or worse? When people act instinctively, they are likely to reflect their character and personality: to become aggressive, to go into their shell, to mumble something incoherent, and so on. They are unlikely to cope effectively with the situation. Indeed, they may well make the situation worse, realise this and become stressed, so starting up a vicious circle in which they become less and less able to cope.

66 Even among professional fighters, danger often reduces a man to his most foolish instincts. A true fighter can think his way out of crisis. Cassius Clay really knew how to fight when he was in trouble. He never panicked or forgot what I taught him.[1] 99

❝ He'd take a good punch, and then go right back boxing and box his way out of it, the way I taught him.[2] **❞**

Much the same could be written about good managers. How easy it is for people to fall back on what they usually do or what their character drives them to do – yet if they do, they may well get it wrong and be a poor manager. Wouldn't it have been better if they had been taught how to think their way through their difficulties, like Cassius Clay?

Which poses another question. What it is that good managers do? What have they learnt that gives them a basis for solving their managerial problems? The answer can be found in our principles for the better manager to follow: what we call our "virtues for managing."

Contents of This Book

In the next chapter, we describe each of these virtues and give examples of how they are used, contrasting what good managers do with what poor managers do. Our aim is to give readers a clear understanding of the meaning and importance of each virtue, along with anecdotes and illustrations that will help them remember the virtue and, we hope, pass it on to others.

To be of any real value, the virtues have to give managers in real situations credible answers to the question "What do I do next?" In chapter 3, we consider six different situations drawn from real life, taking each virtue in turn to generate ideas about possible actions. We draw these steps together to construct a way forward that is consistent with all the virtues. By reading the examples, you will see how to use the virtues so that you will be able to apply them to your situation in accordance with your own values and preferences. The best answer to any problem will depend on a whole range of factors; all we are attempting to do is to find solutions that are consistent with being a great manager.

Chapter 4 considers how you can make yourself a better manager by improving your use of the virtues. We suggest you conduct a self-assessment to see how far your management actions are already consistent with the virtues of managing, using the checklists in the appendix. This will allow you to identify your own needs and to develop a training programme to make you *Simply a Great Manager*.

How to Use This Book

One way to use this book is to read the book from cover to cover and learn the virtues one by one – in other words, to treat it as a textbook.

The second option is to treat it as a reference guide that you can dip in and out of when you are stuck: "Let's see what Hoyle and Newman say!" We hope you'll find inspiration from our text as well as from the many quotations we have used to illustrate the virtues.

You can also use the book as a training manual. By working through the self-assessment forms, you can gain an idea of your weaknesses in the use of the virtues of managing, and then rectify them by studying the relevant sections from chapter 2. After a while, you can use the self-assessment forms again to assess how much improvement you have made.

Finally, we hope that this book will be seen as a contribution to the discipline of managing. This is not a culture, nor an ethos, but a means of generating a good solution out of all the diverse possibilities that a particular situation presents. We would like to think that *Simply a Great Manager* provides a methodology for solving the problems managers encounter every day, no matter who they are and no matter what the circumstances.

02

The Virtues of Great Managers

In this chapter we set out the virtues that we believe all great managers possess. In describing them, we have made use of many proverbs and sayings. We hope that at least one of them will strike a chord with you and that you will use that phrase as a constant reminder to follow the virtue in every managerial situation you face. As you read the chapter, you may like to note down your favourite sayings on a sheet of paper and keep it in a convenient place, such as your palmtop, diary or personal organiser. Not only will it act as a constant reminder of the virtues, but it will also be at hand when you encounter tricky situations in the future.

Let's now look at each of the fifteen virtues.

1 Having the Courage to Confront Situations

Many of the difficult situations that managers find themselves in arise because something isn't going to plan, or because something disagreeable has happened. The manager is faced with deciding what to do.

One option is to ignore the problem and do nothing. Imagine your boss gives you yet another job to do before you go home. You shrug your shoulders and get on with it, even though you have promised your partner you will be home on time tonight. That's the response of a poor manager.

The good manager says, "I have a problem. I need to do something about it. I can't allow this sort of situation to arise. I need to talk to my manager, or my partner. Maybe I need to do something else as well." You don't run away or bury your head in the sand; instead, you decide to talk to your boss with a view to finding a solution to what you see as a problem.

What a good manager actually does in this situation depends on many factors, as we see in chapter 3 when we consider how to deal with a range of real situations. For the moment, the point is that the better manager will have the courage to confront the situation: you will go and talk to your boss and/or your partner.

Many sayings and aphorisms describe this most important virtue for managing:

> 66 Courage is rightly esteemed the first of all human qualities because it is the quality that guarantees all others. 99
>
> *Winston Churchill*

66 The only thing necessary for the triumph of evil is for good men to do nothing. 99

Edmund Burke, Irish philosopher

66 If you want to make peace, you don't talk to your friends; you talk to your enemies. 99

Legendary Middle East military leader

66 To know how to refuse is as important as to know how to consent. 99

Baltasar Grecian, Spanish writer and priest

66 One person with courage makes a majority. 99

Lieutenant General Andrew Jackson

66 An appeaser is one who feeds a crocodile, hoping it will feed on him last. 99

Winston Churchill

66 The truth of the matter is that you always know the right thing to do. The hard thing is to do it. 99

General Norman Schwarzkopf

66 Always do right. This will gratify some people and astonish the rest. 99

Mark Twain

❝ Bite the bullet. **❞**

Anon

❝ Never grow a wishbone, daughter, where your backbone should be. **❞**

Clementine Paddleford, American journalist

You may find it helpful to choose one or two of these sayings to help you remember the virtue. You can write them – or the virtue itself – on a piece of card and use it as a bookmark in your diary. It's important not only to remember and understand the virtue, but to know how to use it in practice. Managers with courage:

✓ Are open and easy to talk to, and willing to talk.
✓ Like all the cards on the table. They have no hidden agendas.
✓ Call a spade a spade.
✓ Are self-critical. They know where the buck stops: with them.

By contrast, the behaviour of managers who lack courage is characterised by:

✗ Running away from difficult situations.
✗ Addressing the symptoms, not the causes.
✗ Sweeping things under the carpet.
✗ Talking only to those who agree with them.
✗ Blaming others for their predicament.

Good managers recognise that a problem exists, and

accept that where it involves them they have some part to play in resolving it. It's interesting to note that these characteristics appear as the first two steps to managing yourself back to good mental health in Paul Hewitt's book *So You Think You're Mad*:

Step One: Problem recognition and identification ...

Step Two: Acceptance and resolution. Accepting a problem relinquishes stubbornness and pride, those afflictions that often stop someone from ever getting the help they so desperately need. Once acceptance sets in, there is the resulting resolution: the resolve to actually do something about one's mental problem.[3]

The senior managers of Barings Bank would have avoided the whole Leeson debacle and the bank's subsequent closure if they had confronted each other and the relevant financial authorities with all that they knew about the bank's exposure and losses. Instead, they chose to operate a conspiracy of silence, with disastrous results for the bank and themselves.

By contrast, Lieutenant General Michael Jackson knew what he should say, and said it. Just as the NATO bombing campaign in Kosovo ceased in 1999, his commanding officer, General Wesley Clark, ordered him to block the runway at Pristina, the provincial capital, to prevent Moscow reinforcing a small force of troops that had occupied the airfield. General Jackson defied his superior, famously telling him, "Sir, I am not starting World War III for you!"

One of the most difficult situations for managers comes when they realise that they themselves are the problem that needs to be addressed. This happened to the chairman of a firm of consultants. One of the directors, a man named Geoffrey, saw that the business needed to transform itself if it was to avoid disaster. He convinced the chairman that change was vital and that he – the chairman – was part of the problem. So the chairman called a staff meeting to make his announcement: "Geoffrey here is going to help us change the way we do things. And he's going to start with me!"

This announcement sent a clear signal to the whole company. The company was stuck in a rut. Its management had become set in its ways. The chairman meant business, and he recognised that he himself had to change if he was to stop being part of the problem and become part of the solution. What's more, he had the courage and good grace to admit it publicly.

There is an obvious moral in this anecdote for anyone who aspires to be a successful manager.

Shows Courage.

2 Understanding Your Priorities

A common failing of managers is trying to do too much. Poor managers don't focus on their priorities. As a result, they are always short of time, they miss deadlines, and they leave unpleasant things until tomorrow, which never comes. Their output is often superficial, or poorly executed.

How easy it is to focus on the wrong thing: to be concerned with matters that aren't really that important, or to waste time, energy and resources addressing the wrong issues. How frustrating for staff not to know what their manager wants them to do first, and what can wait until later. How frustrating for the management team to wait for a colleague to complete trivial tasks before taking on much more important work.

Good managers concentrate on their priorities: the things that are *really* important. They recognise that priorities need to be re-evaluated, and they do this regularly and often.

A number of sayings and quotations reflect this virtue for managing:

66 First things first. **99**

Proverb

66 Our greatest danger in life is permitting the urgent things to crowd out the important. **99**

Charles Hummel, American writer

66 I have learnt that lack of focus is the most common cause of corporate mediocrity. **99**

Louis Gerstner, former chairman, IBM

66 I shall reproach you for underestimating what is most valuable, and for praising what is unimportant. 99

Socrates

66 There is nothing quite so useless as doing with great efficiency what should not be done at all. 99

Peter Drucker, management guru

66 The bitterness of poor quality is remembered long after the sweetness of a low price has faded away from memory. 99

Aldo Gucci

66 Things that matter most must never be at the mercy of things that matter least. 99

Goethe

An important corollary of focusing on your priorities is *not* spending time on low-priority items. Otherwise the available hours in the day will be spread too thinly for you to achieve real progress in any of them.

Good managers identify and focus on the important things, and ignore the rest. If they don't have the time to do everything they need to do, they delegate the less important tasks. They apply the 80/20 rule: 80% of the results you are seeking can often be achieved by doing just 20% of everything that could be done.

Good managers:

✓ Stop and think before they start work every morning or begin a new project.
✓ Identify the important things and then tackle them in priority order.
✓ May miss some deadlines, but never the most important ones.
✓ Always seem to work within their capacity – busy, but never too busy.
✓ Negotiate with their bosses over what to focus on.

Poor managers:

✗ Mistake activity for effectiveness. Busyness is not good business.
✗ Tend to leave the most important tasks until last, often because they are the hardest.
✗ Chop and change between tasks, working on a bit of this and a bit of that.
✗ Often miss important deadlines.
✗ Complain they have too much work and not enough time.
✗ Never say no to doing more work.

We once knew a chief executive of a computer services company who was keen on attending evening functions in order to develop business contacts and gather commercial intelligence. He called his executives together three times a week to brief them on what he had learnt. He would tell them about his latest business idea and ask them to explore its potential and prepare an outline development plan. Unfortunately, there was never enough time to complete the work on one idea before another one came along. Because they failed to allocate priorities, the team couldn't complete the work on even a few worthwhile ideas. Needless to say, the company never achieved the move into new business areas that it needed to make.

Priorities are usually thought of in terms of time. What is the most important thing for me to focus on in the next minute, hour, day, week, month, year? After all, we have a finite amount of time: just 24 hours in a day, 7 days in a week. And once a period of time has gone, you can't get it back again; that's it.

Financial resources should be seen in much the same way. What should be our priorities for using our income and savings, including the money tied up in our house and other assets? How do these priorities compare with the way we are actually using these resources? Successful managers of a family or business budget resolve conflicts over their use of money as well as time.

3 Knowing Your Objectives

Good managers know what they are trying to achieve, whether it is with their company, family, or whatever. They may use a variety of different words to describe the desired outcome of their actions: objective, vision, goal, aim, target, dream. They know their long-term, medium-term and short-term objectives, and they prioritise them to avoid any conflicts.

Here are a few sayings to help you remember this important virtue.

66 To tend unfailingly towards a goal is the secret of success. 99

Anna Pavlova, Russian ballerina

66 If you don't know where you are going, any road will take you there. 99

Philip Kotler, marketing expert

66 You ask, what is our aim? I can answer in one word: victory... . Victory at all costs, victory in spite of all the terror, victory however long and hard the road may be; for without victory there is no survival. 99

Winston Churchill

66 If one does not know to which port one is sailing, no wind is favourable. 99

Seneca

"I have a dream."

Martin Luther King

"Failure is no disgrace, low aim is."

Michael Howells, film production designer

"Man's reach should exceed his grasp."

Robert Browning

"For whatever profession, your inner devotion to the task you have set yourself must be so deep that you can never be deflected from your aim."

Walter Gropius, architect

Good managers:

- ✓ Clarify and review their objectives regularly, checking that they are still appropriate.
- ✓ Constantly use their objectives as a point of reference, especially when the going gets tough or things are uncertain.
- ✓ Write their aims down and discuss them with everyone who will be affected by them.
- ✓ Want to know the objectives of meetings.
- ✓ Often ask, "What are we trying to achieve?"
- ✓ Use their objectives to measure progress and the success of their actions.

Poor managers:

- ✗ Are vague about what they want to achieve.
- ✗ Find it difficult to make up their mind.
- ✗ Make decisions on the basis of a variety of criteria that often change.
- ✗ Make inconsistent decisions.
- ✗ Lack focus in their work and activities.

If you don't define your objectives, anything you achieve is pure luck and of uncertain value to you. How can you plan to do anything unless you know your objectives? When managers do something inappropriate, it's often because they have failed to define their objectives correctly.

This also applies to parents. At one moment they may be keen to discipline their children; at another, they may give in to them for the sake of peace and quiet. This confuses the child, and neither instills discipline nor creates a real bond.

We once attended an outdoor concert at a country estate on a lovely Sunday evening. The organisers had booked some excellent soloists to perform with a top orchestra. Great care had been taken with the route for cars, and with the parking. The stage was at the top of a hill so that everyone could see what was going on. Perfect, you might think. Sadly not. Because the orchestra was at the top of the hill, the music floated away over the audience's heads. The organisers had failed to satisfy the prime objective of the concert-goers: to hear the music.

Always check that you know the objectives of your client, partner or whoever. If you get it wrong, it will make a big difference to the effectiveness of your actions. One of us had an uncle who made office furniture. Not long after starting up his business, he was delighted to receive a trial order for stools from the owner of a coffee shop in central London. He worked hard to make the metal frame elegant but strong, and the seat perfectly upholstered. Imagine his disappointment when the owner rang to ask him to take the stools away. "What's wrong with them?" "They're too comfortable – the girls come in for lunch and sit on them for ages while they smoke their cigarettes. It's bad for business. But you can have the order if you make them a little bit uncomfortable!"

A well-defined objective is like a flag in a battlefield, showing everyone the direction to follow. Imagine three men rowing a boat with no destination in mind. First they will have to argue about where they are going, and even when they have agreed their rowing may still be untidy. But if they have a sense of shared purpose from the outset, they will work in harmony and make rapid progress.

4 Listening and Learning

How many times have you encountered managers who would be far more effective if they were to listen more? How much more could be done if bosses would only pay attention to their subordinates? How much better would a manager's decisions be if they were based on an appreciation of *all* the relevant information?

Most managers would agree that it is important to listen and learn from others. But an outstanding manager is one who not only understands this often underrated virtue but actually puts it into practice.

There are many sayings to remind us of this virtue:

66 We have two ears and one mouth so that we can listen twice as much as we speak. 99

Epictetus, Greek philosopher

66 Wise people speak when they have something to say; foolish people speak because they have to say something. 99

Todd Hafer, American author

66 A wise person hears one word and understands two. 99

Yiddish proverb

66 The most important thing in communicating is to hear what isn't being said. 99

Peter Drucker

❝Do you listen to your neighbour? Do you know when he needs help?**❞**
Mother Teresa of Calcutta

❝Why are we telling the peasants what to do? We should be listening to them.**❞**
Tolstoy

Listening involves much more than hearing. We need to understand the complete meaning. Looking at a person is like looking at an iceberg; we don't see beneath the surface. We can see how someone behaves, but their feelings, opinions, personality, values, beliefs, attitudes, knowledge and experience are hidden from view.

Another important aspect of listening is whom you listen to – and it shouldn't necessarily be the people who make the most noise.

Good managers:
- ✓ Listen more than they talk.
- ✓ Aren't too proud to ask for advice.
- ✓ Look for feedback on their performance.
- ✓ Explore ideas with other people.

Poor managers:
- ✗ Are impulsive.
- ✗ Think they know the answer.
- ✗ Have the "not invented here" syndrome.
- ✗ Are cocksure, or lack confidence.
- ✗ Have inflated ideas about their own experience.

A story tells of an army platoon weaving through a jungle towards a safe base camp. The trail is long, with many twists and turns. The leader has a gun, a map and a captain's insignia. Soon the platoon reaches a fork in the path. The captain shouts, "This way, chaps, the safe way to the camp is on the left." At the back of the platoon is Private Brown, who has been along the path before. He has no stripes on his shoulder, and no gun. He calls out, "Wait a minute, boys, I've been along here before. The safe way is on the right. The left fork is infested with enemy snipers and booby traps."

Whom do you follow? Rank or experience? A truly effective captain would take into account the experience of his subordinates. If he had asked his team before setting out whether anyone had been there before, he could have developed an effective solution. By tapping the resources of his men he would have demonstrated how much he trusts them in a threatening situation. His authority would then derive not from his rank, but from his knowledge and the trust his colleagues place in him.

Listens and learns.

5 Knowing Yourself

One of the more subtle virtues of good managers is that they know themselves. They know what they are good at, and they certainly know what they are bad at. They are able to achieve things by drawing on their strengths and steering clear of their weaknesses. They know that their reputation and authority as good managers spring from doing things well, and if they fail to do things well they will destroy both.

Good managers have humility and recognise the need to work with others. They never ignore their weaknesses but take steps to deal with them, perhaps through an active learning programme or a period of training.

So let's look at a few quotes that deal with this important virtue:

66 A fault is a crack, gradually widening and separating people. 99

Jung

66 There is none so foolish as the one who thinks himself or herself abundantly wise. 99

Todd Hafer

66 Your true character is revealed by what you do when no one is watching. 99

Todd Hafer

❝ The fault, dear Brutus, is not in our stars, but in ourselves. **❞**

Cassius in Julius Caesar

❝ You should be able to spot the sucker at the table right away. If you can't, it must be you. **❞**

Poker player's maxim

❝ There is never a failure of talent, only of character. **❞**

Ernest Hemingway

❝ His only weakness is that he thinks he doesn't have one. **❞**

Arsène Wenger on Sir Alex Ferguson

❝ This above all: to thine own self be true
And it must follow, as the night the day
Thou canst not then be false to any man. **❞**

Polonius to his son Laertes in Hamlet

❝ At times of crisis, we are left on our own. **❞**

Pope Benedict XVI

Good managers:

✓ Are realistic about their abilities.
✓ Admit their shortcomings.

✓ Are happy to delegate.
✓ Ask for help from others.

Poor managers:
✗ Try to tackle everything.
✗ Bite off more than they can chew.
✗ Tend to be self absorbed.
✗ Act beyond their competence and experience.

It isn't easy to know yourself, or to know how others perceive you. As Robbie Burns put it:

❝ Oh, to see ourselves as others see us. **❞**

The key is to:

❝ *Never ignore the feeling in your bones.* **❞**
Darrol Stinton, test pilot

Every time you think you have made a success of something, or someone congratulates you on an achievement, ask yourself exactly what it was that you did. Perhaps you gained the confidence of two colleagues who were arguing; you understood the feelings of your teenage daughter; or you thought through the consequences of having a row with your son about his girlfriend. If you do this frequently, after a while you will begin to build up a picture of things you are good at.

Similarly, when you know you have handled a situation

badly or feel uneasy about something, ask yourself why. Perhaps your concentration wandered during a meeting you weren't very interested in and you got caught out, or you made a fool of yourself by jumping in with an answer only to be corrected by someone who knew more about the subject than you did. Was it your difficulty with numbers that made you so reticent yesterday when your boss was discussing your group's financial results? If you are honest with yourself, after a while you will build up an accurate picture of your weaknesses by following this little routine.

Finally, we should remember that, in the words of a famous American journalist, Ed Murrow,

> 66 Everyone is a prisoner of his own experience. No one can eliminate prejudices – just recognise them. 99

We should always bear this in mind when we try to know ourselves.

6 Believing in Teams

The saying "May the best team win" means more than might appear at first sight. People usually take it to mean that the side with the best players should triumph, but it should also be taken as meaning that victory should go to the side that exhibits the best teamwork.

There are many sayings about team and teamwork:

66 The way a team plays as a whole determines its success. You may have the greatest bunch of individual stars in the world, but if they don't play together, the club won't be worth a dime. 99

Babe Ruth, US baseball star

66 The greatest quality that an individual can possess is the ability to get along with others. It is a quality that I am willing to pay more for than any other. 99

Andrew Carnegie

66 Sticks in a bundle are unbreakable. 99

Kenyan proverb

66 If we do not hang together, we shall hang – together. 99

Anon

❝Two are better than one, because they have a good return for their work: if one falls down, his friend can help him up. But pity the man who falls and has no one to help him up.**❞**

Ecclesiastes 4:9–10

❝Global problems can be solved without any one person having a global view. Think what ants do!**❞**

Steven Johnson, American writer

❝The difference between mediocrity and greatness is the feeling these guys have for each other. Most people call it team spirit.**❞**

Vince Lombardi, football coach

❝You can't clap with one hand.**❞**

Jewish proverb

❝Make sure everybody counts and everybody knows they count.**❞**

Jack Welch, former CEO, GE

❝There is no "I" in team.**❞**

Montreal Canadiens ice hockey team

Good managers:
- ✓ Share their problems.
- ✓ Offer to help their staff.

✓ Ask others for their views and are happy to discuss their own.
✓ Use the skills of their staff.
✓ Will accept the consensus of their teams.
✓ Invest time to get to know their staff.
✓ Practise give and take.

Poor managers:
✗ Are loners.
✗ Keep things to themselves.
✗ Aren't keen on having meetings with their staff.
✗ Have superficial relationships with their staff.

At one multinational oil company, the recently appointed chairman was asked how he had achieved his success. He said that he got there on the back of the people who worked for him. He made sure they were well trained; he supported them; they worked together to solve problems; and when he got promoted, he made sure they were promoted too. Not surprisingly, his team stuck by him, because they could see where he was taking them.

As Peter Drucker says,

❝ No matter what the textbooks and organisation charts say, well-managed companies do not have a one-man chief executive. They have an executive team. ❞

Good managers value their teams not only because a team can produce much more than the sum of its individual members' contributions, but also because a team provides a framework that can give satisfaction to its members. Each individual can experience a share in a success that they might never be able to achieve on their own, as this anecdote illustrates.

One of us was fortunate to have a son at a school whose headmaster followed this ethic. He recognised that some boys were known for being good at sport, others at music, yet others at art, and so on. But there were some who weren't known for anything in particular. He went out of his way to make sure they did something that was important to the school. For example, when parents of prospective pupils came to visit, he gave these "unknowns" the job of showing them around the school. They were thrilled: here was something they would be known for doing. They developed a pride in their work because the head valued them and they did not want to let him down.

Within the framework of a team, there is a role for everyone and scope for each of us to succeed and be seen to succeed.

Team work works!

7 Believing in Delegation

It is impossible for managers always to do everything themselves. If they insist on performing every task they are responsible for, they will be overworked. They will become a bottleneck, miss deadlines, and complete tasks superficially or incompletely. Instead of doing the job properly, they will focus on finishing tasks as soon as possible.

One managing director who couldn't delegate brought his company to a standstill. Whenever he went on holiday, no decisions were made. After a while, the factory stopped operating. No one had bought any raw materials; it was something the boss always dealt with and had never delegated.

Delegation has to be clear in terms of the focus and the boundaries of what is being delegated: what can be done and what can't be done. When you delegate, you are asking somebody to do something on your behalf, but that doesn't absolve you from responsibility. It is no good saying, "Oh, sorry I didn't do what I was supposed to do, but I asked X to do it and he let me down."

A story from about 2,000 years ago illustrates the true meaning of delegation. In the Roman Empire, a new governor of a province travelled to Rome to be briefed on its political system and the rules under which he was to operate. He was told how far his powers extended and what the emperor wanted him to achieve.

Off he went to his house in the provincial capital. He didn't return for ten years. During that time, there was no contact between the emperor and the governor apart from a few messages. The emperor was still responsible for the administration of the empire, but he had delegated to the governor the job of running a large part of it.

A few sayings help to illuminate this important virtue:

66 The ability to delegate is a busy person's wealth. 99

Taylor Morgan

66 Hire people cleverer than you are and delegate more than you think good for you. And take the blame. 99

Peter Parker, British businessman

66 I not only use all the brains I have, but all I can borrow. 99

Woodrow Wilson

66 I learnt ... how to take hold of something by letting go. 99

Arsène Wenger

66 Surround yourself with the best people you can find, delegate authority, and don't interfere. 99

Ronald Reagan

66 If you give people responsibility they will tend to be responsible; if you take it away they will tend to be irresponsible. 99

Norman Tebbit, UK politician

66 Never ask anybody to do anything you would not do yourself. 99

Allen Shepherd, leading British manager

Good managers:
- ✓ Actively delegate.
- ✓ Have confidence in their staff.
- ✓ Leave their door open.
- ✓ Always take responsibility for the performance of their teams.

Poor managers:
- ✗ Are bottlenecks: everyone waits for them to finish their work.
- ✗ Work excessively long hours.
- ✗ Don't know what their staff are capable of.

Delegation is also a training tool; it can be used to try people out. Parents give little jobs to their children and then help them when they can't quite do everything they want to do. Delegation motivates people too. We like it when our bosses give us jobs to do. It shows they trust us and have confidence in us. Perhaps they aren't the most important or enjoyable tasks, but they are a beginning. If we do small things well we can hope to be trusted with something bigger. Delegation is part of the process of developing people, another of our virtues.

However, delegating is not the same as giving orders. Issuing very detailed instructions is a poor way to practise delegation. Consider the words of General George Patton:

> 66 Never tell people how to do things. Tell them what you want them to achieve and they will surprise you with their ingenuity. 99

Similarly, when you are delegating, don't ask lots of questions about how the work was carried out unless they are both relevant and useful. It's a waste of time for all involved and undermines the confidence of the person who has done the job. Trust people, especially if they have achieved what you asked them to do.

8 Knowing the Value of Time

Two of the commonest phrases in management are "If only I had the time" and "I haven't got the time." The usual response is "Then make the time." But this is impossible. Time can't be created, stored, saved up or bought. Time is a resource, but it is of value only if we use it well. Or to put it another way, time is only well spent if it produces something of value.

All we know is that there are 24 hours in a day and we have to decide how to spend them. One major oil company used the slogan: *"Clear your desk and leave on time."* The implication was clear: if you couldn't achieve what you were supposed to achieve in an eight-hour day, you were probably doing the wrong things and not delegating enough, and you might be in the wrong job as well.

If we decide where we want to spend our time, we also decide implicitly where we *don't* want to spend it. The trouble is that this is a subconscious decision. The trick is to make it conscious: to say deliberately to yourself, "I won't do this because it isn't worth the time involved and I have more important things to do." And then, of course, you must do them. [4]

Wasting time often reflects other problems: failing to delegate; disregarding your own priorities; having the wrong priorities; having poorly trained staff; not being in control of situations so that you are always facing a crisis; or finding it difficult to make decisions.

Memorable sayings about the value of time include:

66 Procrastination is the thief of time. 99

Edward Young, poet

66 Time is nature's way keeping everything from happening at once. 99

Anon

66 Time and tide wait for no man. 99

Proverb

66 There is always time if one uses it well. 99

Goethe

66 To choose time is to save time. 99

Francis Bacon

66 If you are too busy to help those around you succeed, you are too busy. 99

Anon

66 The lack of time is not a problem; it is a symptom. 99

Martin Scott, consultant

66 What is past is gone. What is important is what lies ahead. 99

Tony Adams, Arsenal and England football captain

66 Time is money – use it wisely. 99

Anon

Good managers:

✓ Always seem to have time.
✓ Find time to do something extra, if it is really important.
✓ Seem to meet their deadlines.
✓ Don't automatically say, "I'll do it."
✓ Are open about budgeting their time and keep a detailed diary of all their plans.

Poor managers:

✗ Miss their deadlines.
✗ Take shortcuts.
✗ Are usually late for appointments.
✗ Chair meetings that overrun.
✗ Spend time on unproductive activities not linked to their priorities or objectives.
✗ Leave things to the last moment.

David Gower, the former captain of the English cricket team, is a good example of someone who knew the value of time. He gave himself time to play the right shot. He'd keep still, wait for the ball and play it as it needed to be played, usually with great results.

Timing is also vital in telling jokes, of course. Great comics are masters of timing.

Making the best use of the time available to you is not just about deciding what to do; it is also about waiting for the *best time* to do things:

❝ Timing is everything. **❞**

Imagine you need to reprimand someone. It's usually best to do this at the first opportunity when the two of you are alone. Don't wait for your staff member to repeat the offending behaviour, or – worse – tell them off the next time you meet if there are other people present.

The best reason not to rush in and do something is that you always need to stop and think. Is this the right thing to do? Is this the right time? What is the downside? Once you have acted, you can't undo what you have done. That time has passed.

9 Believing in People Development

We take it for granted that our children need to go to school to be educated. As parents, we recognise that part of our responsibility to our sons and daughters is to prepare them for their life ahead. But being able to read and write or understand the fundamentals of physics or summon historical facts are not the only important things. Children need to be prepared for many other aspects of life: recognising danger, being sociable, being polite, being honest, being able to share and take turns.

Developing people consists of passing on what we might call "soft" knowledge as well as "hard" knowledge. Hard knowledge is the kind of thing you can look up in a book, or be tested on in an exam – an answer to a specific question. Who was the first man to walk on the moon? Where did Christopher Columbus begin his voyage to America? How do you wire a plug on a lamp? Why does a magnet always point in the same direction?

Soft knowledge is something you have to find out for yourself. It comes from experience. One example is the way children learn to be sociable and find out that letting other children play with their toys makes everyone much happier. Good parents and teachers provide the motivation and discipline for children to begin to understand that sharing is good, and that it is different from giving.

By contrast, consider the mother who answers for her little girl when an interested grown-up tries to start a conversation. "How old are you?" "She's three." It's hardly surprising that the mother can talk and knows her numbers. Her priority, however, should be to develop her child, not to answer for her. The question was asked not to learn the answer, but to invite the child to speak. The fact that we know the answer doesn't mean we have to provide it. Sometimes we need to allow or help others to answer.

It is a simple step to say that if parents should develop their children, then managers should develop their staff – the people for whom they are responsible. This makes good sense for a number of reasons. It will prepare them to do the tasks you want to delegate to them; it will train them to do your job when you are no longer doing it; it will make them more efficient and less likely to make mistakes; and you owe it to them to pass on your knowledge so that they can develop as people and reach their full potential.

There are many sayings about the importance of developing people:

> 66 The greatest good you can do for others is not just to share your riches, but to reveal them as their own. 99
>
> *Disraeli*

> 66 Rebuke a wise man and he will love you. Instruct a wise man and he will be wiser still. 99
>
> *Proverbs 9:8–9*

> 66 A candle loses nothing of its light by lighting another candle. 99
>
> *James Keller, Catholic priest*

❝ Give a man a fish and you feed him for a day. Teach a man to fish and you feed him for a lifetime. **❞**

Chinese proverb

❝ The good captain enables talent to flower. Like a gardener, he must not prune too hard; nor can he leave it all to nature. **❞**

Mike Brearley, former England cricket captain

Good managers:
- ✓ Like helping people to solve problems.
- ✓ See tasks undertaken by their staff as an opportunity to develop them.
- ✓ Don't do things for others, but help them do things themselves.
- ✓ Realise that in developing others they are developing themselves and building a more capable team.

Poor managers:
- ✗ Think training is for the training department.
- ✗ Rob the training budget of the time and money that has been set aside.
- ✗ Believe that showing their staff how to do something is a waste of time when they can do it faster themselves.

It is a mistake to think that only those at the top of an organisation are worth developing, or that managers should do only enough training to remain "superior" to all those who work in their group.[5] Consider the inscription on the tombstone of Andrew Carnegie, a highly successful American businessman in the early part of the twentieth century:

> 66 Here lies a man who knew how to enlist in his service better men than himself. 99

Developing people always means training them, but not necessarily through formal training courses. During the sixteenth century, Galileo wrote:

> 66 You can't teach a man anything, you can only help him to discover things. 99

Louis Pasteur is reputed to have said:

> 66 Chance favours only the trained mind. 99

Most teachers will echo this sentiment. Learning has to come from inside a person. You have to *want* to learn. Lecturing can take people only so far. Personal exploration and discovering things for oneself can yield far better results than listening to those who know or profess to know. After all,

> 66 Example is not the main thing in influencing others, it is the only thing. 99
> *Albert Schweitzer, 1952 Nobel Peace Prize Winner*

There is an ancient Chinese proverb that makes this point well:

> **"**Hear and forget, see and remember, do and understand.**"**

One of our colleagues lectured on finance for years. He was regarded as brilliant at his subject, yet his style of teaching alienated a class of senior managers. He had a deep understanding of financial techniques, but rammed it down their throats in rapid-fire fashion. He once admitted that he couldn't see the value of the case-study approach in which students work through a problem for themselves. In his teaching, he had failed to identify his true objective: to have students learn, not to deliver a lecture or show how clever he was.

An important part of learning is practice. Gary Player, the outstanding South African golfer, was asked at a press conference whether golf was a matter of luck. He replied:

> **"**Sure it is. The only thing is, the more I practise, the luckier I get.[6]**"**

Another witty commentator, Bob Monkhouse, made a similar point:

> **"**The formula for success is where preparation meets opportunity.**"**

❝ Good managers arrange or provide suitable training because they understand its value: Training is an investment, not a cost. **❞**

As Dean Bok of Harvard University said:

❝ If you think training is expensive, try ignorance! **❞**

The Developer

10 Being a Motivator

The British social reformer and Labour minister Lord Beveridge is credited with saying that the task of management is "To make common men do uncommon things." That might include encouraging shop assistants to work at the checkout when they would rather be going home, or encouraging your children to do their homework when they would rather be outside playing with their friends. If managers are to meet their objectives for the groups they are responsible for, then their staff have to do what their manager wants them to do, not what *they* would rather do. The ability to motivate people should be an integral part of every manager's armoury.

Good managers don't rely solely on the power of formal motivational systems such as bonuses and commissions, nor on threats and sanctions such as issuing warnings or withholding pocket money. They know that there are other ways of motivating people: to value them as individuals and not as cogs in a wheel, and to appeal to the pride they take in their work, their need to be wanted, and their wish to be seen as successful. Good managers seldom need to refer to these needs explicitly; rather, they will know their staff well enough to understand what makes them tick and to use that knowledge to their mutual advantage. Even strategy can be used as a motivator:

> 66 Strategy doesn't only have to position; it has to inspire. 99
>
> *Henry Mintzberg, management guru*

People can be motivated in many different ways. Soon after the beginning of World War II, Churchill motivated the British people to overcome the threat of Nazi Germany by saying:

> 66 You ask, what is our aim? I can answer in one word: Victory! 99

He summed up the situation in a single striking phrase, as he did later before the Battle of Britain:

> 66 Let us therefore brace ourselves to our duties, and so bear ourselves that if the British Empire and its Commonwealth last for a thousand years, men will say: 'This was their finest hour.' 99

At his inauguration, US president John F. Kennedy said:

> 66 Ask not what your country can do for you, but what you can do for your country. 99

His words live on because they sum up a complex array of ideas and emotions in a few well-chosen words. The young president was challenging the conventional politics of his day and providing inspiration for Americans in the years that followed.

If these utterances had been longer, they would not have been so memorable. It is no accident that the Lord's Prayer is 56 words long and the Gettysburg Address 121 words. George Bernard Shaw captured the idea when he wrote:

> 66 This letter would have been shorter had I had more time. 99

Both Kennedy and Churchill knew the value of crafting memorable phrases that had an immediate impact on people.

Similarly, companies often adopt pithy phrases to sum up their strategy, attract customers and motivate staff:

> 66 We try harder. 99
>
> *Avis*

> 66 You'll feel better with us. 99
>
> *Aetna, a US healthcare company*

These slogans embody the ABC of communication: accuracy, brevity and clarity.

Good managers are able to weigh a situation and articulate the right response in a couple of sentences that are easily remembered and understood. No manager can hope to motivate other people effectively by staying in their office and communicating by email.

Many phrases teach us that effective motivation means treating people with respect:

> 66 To speak kindly does not hurt the tongue. 99
>
> *French proverb*

66 An ounce of leading is worth a pound of pressure. 99

66 Be nice to nerds; chances are you'll end up working for one. 99

Bill Gates

66 A spoonful of honey will catch more flies than a gallon of vinegar. 99

Benjamin Franklin

66 The most practical advice for leaders is not to treat pawns like pawns or princes like princes, but to treat all people like people. 99

James MacGregor Burns, leadership expert

66 See everything; overlook a lot; correct a little. 99

Pope John XXIII

66 It's always worthwhile to make sure others are aware of their worth. 99

Malcolm Forbes, magazine publisher

Good managers:
- ✓ Acknowledge their staff's contribution to the output of the group.
- ✓ Praise or reprimand people fairly.

✓ Distinguish between effort and effect, and between the individual and the task.

✓ Understand that staff value praise and self-fulfilment as well as salary and status.

Poor managers:

✗ Point out what is wrong and harp on it.

✗ Don't treat their staff as individuals.

✗ Praise their staff only occasionally, if ever.

✗ Bully and threaten people.

✗ Steal their staff's ideas and never give them credit for their work.

Remember:

❝Amazing things happen when you make people feel they are valued as individuals, when you dignify their suggestions and their ideas, when you show your respect for them by allowing them to exercise their own wisdom and judgement and discretion.❞

Herb Kelleher, US airline executive

11 Being in Control

If you try to imagine a perfect manager, you may well think of an unflappable planner who is never stressed or overstretched. You may conjure up someone who heeds the immortal words of Corporal Jones in the classic British sitcom *Dads' Army*: "Don't panic!" Nothing is ever achieved by pressing the panic button. All it does is create confusion. You need to be able to keep your nerve in the face of unexpected events and big changes. You must have faith in yourself, your ideas, and your staff.

Being in control means more than not panicking and taking one thing at a time. It also involves having a well-thought-out strategy, enough money, time and people to carry it out, and contingency plans to deal with the unexpected. Consider the description of the great explorer Ernest Shackleton by his first officer on the ship *Endurance*:

> **❝**He had a quick brain and could visualise things ahead, and as far as he could he safeguarded any eventuality that was likely to occur. **❞**

Good managers tell their staff what to do, when, why and how. The military have a few pithy sayings about this:

> **❝**Failing to plan is planning to fail. **❞**

They also refer to the 6 Ps:

> **❝**Proper Planning Prevents Piss-Poor Performance. **❞**

Being in control means having up-to-date information and being in a position to intervene – but only if you need to. Good managers will monitor what is going on both within their group and externally. If something unexpected happens, action follows. Consider a domestic example. If you aren't sure that your teenage daughter is doing her homework, you might want to pay casual visits to her room. If she isn't, she will already know (because you have told her many times before) that no homework means no night out with her friends.

Good plans and careful monitoring lay the foundation for managing by exception (in other words, intervening only when something goes wrong). An independent view and adequate information, provided it is apposite and timely, should provide a sound basis for a chairman to manage the managing director in order to achieve their company's annual plan. Most organisations use systems that combine financial, budgetary and management data to give managers at every level the information they need to maintain control over what they, their staff and the organisation as a whole are doing.

At GEC, the chairman, Arnold Weinstock, held monthly meetings with divisional managers to discuss their performance: what they had sold, what cash they had collected, and what their forward order book looked like. If these measures were satisfactory, he was content; he knew they were in control of their division. And if they were not, he made sure corrective action was taken

Good managers don't micro-manage, though. They

have learned to let go of the reins, yet they know when to pick them up again if disaster looms.

> **❝** I learnt how to take hold of something by letting go. **❞**
>
> *Arsène Wenger*

To be in control of a situation, you have to look beyond the current state of affairs to the longer term to see the big picture. Control is also about *not* doing certain things: making mistakes, saying the wrong thing, speaking before thinking.

In addition, being in control involves managing expectations. We can sum this up in the form of an equation:

Level of Satisfaction = Achievement minus Expectation

Achieving more than you promised will bring praise; achieving less than you promised will bring disappointment. The outcome has as much to do with what you promised (or led people to expect) as with what you actually achieved.

Many sayings allude to the importance of being in control:

> **❝** Forewarned is forearmed. **❞**

> **❝** A stitch in time saves nine. **❞**

66 Every little thing counts in a crisis. 99
Jawaharlal Nehru

66 Thought and forethought give counsel both on living and on achieving success. 99
Baltasar Grecian

66 If you find yourself in a hole, stop digging. 99

66 True genius resides in the capacity for the evaluation of uncertain, hazardous, and conflicting information. 99
Winston Churchill

66 It's better to debate a question without settling it, than to settle it without debating it. 99
Joseph Joubert, French moralist

Good managers:
- ✓ Always want information.
- ✓ Believe in planning, monitoring and following through.
- ✓ Don't panic.
- ✓ Think widely.
- ✓ Take a step at a time, and aren't afraid to move slowly but surely.
- ✓ Realistically evaluate a problem and the time and resources they need to solve it.

Poor managers:

- ✗ Are seasoned in crisis management.
- ✗ Panic easily.
- ✗ Worry about remote or containable eventualities.
- ✗ Spread disillusionment.
- ✗ Abdicate responsibility.
- ✗ Pass the buck.

J. C. Bamford, the founder of British earth-moving equipment manufacturer JCB, had a favourite motto:

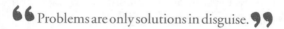 **Problems are only solutions in disguise.**

Good managers adopt a similar attitude. They keep cool heads and make sure they see things clearly, in perspective, and in relation to all the relevant factors. What's more, they are willing to share their thoughts and put doubters and worriers at ease, using logical reasoning and trusting it will see them through.

Control

In Control!

12 Looking for Win+Win Outcomes

A win+win[7] philosophy is one of the greatest weapons for a manager. You can't hope to stay successful if you play for top stakes every time. Things are fine when you are winning, but sooner or later you will lose. At this point, you may not merely forfeit a short-term opportunity, but also sacrifice your team's confidence and support. Much the better strategy is to find a solution that both parties can count as a victory: a win+win outcome.

In business, successful retailers learn not to try and wring maximum advantage from any one negotiation with a supplier. If they achieve a terrific margin by driving the hardest possible bargain, that supplier will probably start losing money and no longer be able to afford to invest in modern systems and designs or keep its key people. It will then cease to provide the very things that attracted the retailer in the first place: a lose+lose outcome.

How many negotiations have broken off or failed because one side felt compelled to push for a particular advantage? Too many people enter a negotiation suspicious of the other party. Suspicion clouds judgement and prompts baseless fears, creating unreasonable perceptions of "them" and unrealistic ideas of "us." The will to come out on top and get what you want is ingrained in many business people at an early age. Determination has its place, but it isn't always the best approach. A long-term view of the big picture can produce a better result for everyone by setting negotiations in a wider context. Too often, an adversarial posture leads to disaster, whereas a win+win attitude produces a calm and productive negotiation culminating in a successful outcome.

On an exercise in Yorkshire, two teams were asked to cross a river using various pieces of equipment. Neither team had enough kit to cross the river alone. After a period of furious competitive activity leading nowhere, one team member approached the other team and asked to borrow a length of rope that they had been trying to use to no effect. The teams quickly realised that a joint effort would allow both of them to achieve their objectives. Here was a graphic example of a win+win outcome. The teams saw the value of cooperation and the ease of reaching a solution when a win+win outcome is sought by both sides.

Another illustration can be seen in the film *The Beautiful Mind*, which tells the story of John Nash, a brilliant mathematician and winner of the Nobel Prize. In a scene where he is lecturing to graduate students, they have trouble hearing him because of the noise from construction work going on just outside the room. So he closes the window. But then a student complains that the room is too hot. Nash replies curtly that he needs to hear his own voice. Another student stands up, goes to the window and opens it. She politely asks the men outside to stop work and returns to her seat. The lecture continues uninterrupted: a win+win for the students and the professor.

Here are various sayings that capture the idea of looking for win+win situations:

❞ You scratch my back, I'll scratch yours. ❞

Anon

66 I don't pay good wages because I have lots of money; I have lots of money because I pay good wages. 99

Robert Bosch, German industrialist

66 The third way, or what Buddhists call the middle way, is not a compromise but more like an apex. 99

Stephen Covery

66 You've got to reach out to the other person. You've got to convince them that long-term friendship should trump short-term adversity. 99

George Bush, Sr

66 Nobody ever sold anything; the task is to help them buy. 99

Martin Scott

66 Two can accomplish more than twice as much as one, for the results can be even better. 99

Ecclesiastes 4:9

66 Good business should contain something for both parties. 99

John Harvey-Jones, British business leader

Good managers:
- ✓ List and explore many options to find a solution.
- ✓ Look at problems from many sides.
- ✓ Put themselves in other people's shoes.
- ✓ Don't regard their opposite number as an enemy.
- ✓ Visualise the impact of their actions on everybody involved.
- ✓ Know that having 50% of something beats having 100% of nothing.
- ✓ Take the time to find out other people's objectives.

Poor managers:
- ✗ Adopt a win–lose attitude: "Ya boo, we win, you lose!"
- ✗ Are selfish and narrow-minded.
- ✗ Are typically concerned with short-term gains at the expense of long-term losses.
- ✗ Have a poor negotiating record.
- ✗ Concentrate on their objectives to the exclusion of all else.

Developing the people in your team is an example of a win+win solution: your staff members improve their skills and at the same time you acquire a stronger team to attack the problems you face. Looking for win+win solutions is a greatly under-used facet of being a good manager. It is well worth cultivating: your actions and decisions will improve, leading to more successful outcomes.

13 Taking Decisions and Sticking to Them

Good managers take decisions, but only when they are ready to do so. They neither vacillate nor lack the courage to do what is needed. They prepare the ground before making their decision: What are the relevant considerations? What information do I have? Do I need more? What analysis do I need to help me reach a decision? What are the realistic options? Which ones best meet my objectives? What are the pros and cons of each one? How is each one likely to turn out, not only in the short term but also over the long term? What are the risks involved? What messages, positive or negative, will each option send to my staff and others?

Only then, once they feel the answer is becoming relatively clear, will good managers make their decision. They may take time to mull over the right decision or deliberately delay in order to think things through, but they never take so long that the lack of a decision creates problems of its own.

The quotations and sayings that sum up the importance of decisiveness include:

> **❝**Nothing is more difficult, and therefore more precious, than to be able to decide. **❞**
>
> *Napoleon Bonaparte*

> **❝**The best thing you can do in my organisation is to make the right decision. The next best thing is to make the wrong decision. What gets you fired is to make no decision.**❞**
>
> *Percy Barnevik, Swedish industrialist*

66 Sit, walk or run; just don't wobble. **99**

Zen saying

66 The only one who never makes a mistake is the one who never does anything. **99**

Theodore Roosevelt

66 This is a hard decision, but I have decided. **99**

President Kennedy during the Cuban missile crisis.

66 The lady's not for turning. **99**

Margaret Thatcher

66 The most common mistake in management decisions is the emphasis on the right answer rather than the right question. **99**

Peter Drucker

Good managers:

✓ Recognise that not making a decision carries a cost...
✓ ... and that it is actually a decision to continue with the present state of affairs.
✓ Aren't trigger-happy.
✓ Make the decision in good time, no sooner or later than it is needed.

Poor managers:

✗ Are afraid of being wrong.

✗ Put decisions off.
✗ Never find time to complete an analysis.
✗ Often suffer from "paralysis by analysis."
✗ Always say they need more information before they can decide.
✗ Blame others for not providing them with the information they need.

Taking a decision is not the only important attribute of a good manager. Sticking to it is crucial too. Nothing undermines a manager's credibility more than chopping and changing. It wastes effort and creates frustration, uncertainty and stress in all concerned. And to be decisive, you also have to follow through your decisions to make sure they have been carried out and have had the effect you intended. Obvious, perhaps, yet most people don't.

Good managers live with their decision too. Of course, if they have failed to collect relevant information or have made a gross error in their analysis, they need to have the courage to own up: "Sorry, I made a mistake. If I'd known that I wouldn't have decided to do X, I'd have decided to do Y." There is no point being bloody-minded and not facing up to reality. Admitting your errors is a welcome sign of humility, but it does cost you a certain amount of credibility; it's best to avoid it by taking care to get your decisions right first time. Remember too that others may suffer from your errors.

14 Being Results-Oriented

Many people are satisfied simply by being busy. They leave no stone unturned; they are remarkable in their diligence and attention to detail; they congratulate themselves on the volume of work they have undertaken. Unfortunately, they mistake activity for achievement. Just doing things adds little to the greater good. It's what your work creates that is important. What did you achieve? What was the end result?

Giving your small children a wash is a good thing if it removes dirt and germs from their hands and faces, but it is an utter waste of time if they are perfectly clean to begin with. In business you see forms being completed, numbers being crunched and so on, but to what purpose? A good manager is interested in the actual *results* of all this effort. It is not the most pleasant of tasks to have to tell someone, "You've worked hard, but what you have been doing is a waste of time; you have created nothing." Yet good managers will do just that because they always look to achieve something that creates value.

Good managers are therefore more interested in measuring outputs than inputs, even if the outputs are more difficult to measure. As John Tukey, an outstanding American statistician, said:

> 66 Far better an approximate answer to the right question, than the exact answer to the wrong question. 99

Good managers start every meeting not with the question

"What are we going to talk about?" but with the question "What do we want to achieve at this meeting?" Such a focus may be uncomfortable, but it distinguishes good managers from bad. A bad sales rep, for instance, will focus on building a relationship and understanding the customer's needs in the hope that a sale will follow. A good sales rep meets a potential customer with the intention of getting an order there and then; finding out about the customer is simply part of the process of securing the order, not an end in itself.

Good managers won't stop until they achieve a positive result from their work. They aren't interested in activity for its own sake. They don't start by stating the reasons why they might fail or why the task is difficult; instead, they say there are a number of obstacles to overcome. They aren't deterred when they find an obstacle is bigger or more persistent than they thought. They work hard and think harder.

Good managers also know the danger of falling between two stools. They don't try to achieve so many things that they can't find the time, energy or resources to do any of them justice. Much better to admit failure with some things at the outset and then focus on achieving results in a limited number of others.

There are a number of sayings and quotations that emphasise the importance of achieving results, including:

> 66 Consider the postage stamp: its usefulness consists in the ability to stick to one thing till it gets there. 99
>
> *Josh Billings, US writer and humorist*

66 Don't argue about the difficulties. The difficulties will argue for themselves. **99**

Winston Churchill

66 It is not hard to fail, but it is worse never to have tried to succeed. **99**

Theodore Roosevelt

66 Our greatest glory is not in never falling, but in rising every time we fall. **99**

Confucius

66 Unless you put yourself on the line and give it your best shot, you'll never know what you could achieve. **99**

Paula Radcliffe, champion runner

66 Edison had 1,500 attempts at inventing the light bulb. **99**

Colin Pillinger, spacecraft expert

66 Obstacles are those frightening things you see when you take your eyes off the goal. **99**

Henry Ford

66 Nothing is impossible; some things are just more difficult. **99**

Egyptian saying

66 You may have to fight a battle more than once to win it. 99

Margaret Thatcher

66 A journey of a thousand miles begins with a single step. 99

Lao Tzu, Chinese philosopher

Good managers:
✓ Are focused on their target.
✓ Are determined.
✓ Concentrate on the ends, not the means.
✓ Look for different ways to overcome difficulties.
✓ Follow through to make sure their decisions are carried out.
✓ Focus on the impact of their actions.
✓ Monitor the actions taken to achieve an objective, and adjust them as necessary.

Poor managers:
✗ Think in terms of doing things.
✗ Are satisfied to have done everything they could have done, regardless of outcome.
✗ Are content to follow accepted practices.
✗ Don't understand the value of delivering on time.
✗ Are noted for the perfection of reports or correspondence that never reach a conclusion.
✗ Don't know the value of the question "So what?" – and never ask it.

In 2003 the England rugby team won the World Cup. By then, they were very results-oriented, but it is interesting to read what Will Carling, a former England captain, said about their performance two years earlier:

> 66 The failure to have achieved results does not come from a lack of talent; they have that in abundance. Neither does it come from poor coaching... . It comes from a willingness to live in the comfort zone and the weakness to blame others rather than accept responsibility... . If England wants to be the best, they need to accept what it takes to be the best. It takes responsibility, it takes honesty, it takes humility and, above all, it takes attitude. 99

Try, try again

15 Being Imaginative

Good managers come up with solutions to a problem by thinking beyond the constraints of a seemingly intractable situation and outside the boundaries of straightforward logic. In other words, they use their imagination. As Albert Einstein once said:

> **"**Imagination is more important than knowledge.... .The important thing is never to stop questioning.**"**

Rudyard Kipling suggested how we might do this:

> **"**I keep six honest serving-men
> (They taught me all I knew)
> Their names are What and Why and When
> And How and Where and Who.**"**

How often do we admire managers who make a problem so much easier by looking at it from another viewpoint? "What business are we in?" is a good example of a simple question that needs to be answered intelligently and imaginatively by all businesses. We like the statement of intent adopted by a French perfumery:

> **"**In the factory, we make perfume; but in the shop, we sell hope.**"**

This ground-breaking idea had far-reaching implications

for the company's sales and marketing. Its promotions stopped talking about what was in the bottle, and focused instead on what it meant to the user. They started to sell the product's benefits, not its features.

Department stores grew once they realised that they were offering an experience rather than simply purveying goods. Successful restaurants know they are providing an occasion, not just a meal.

A number of sayings and quotations bear witness to the power of imagination:

66 Dream no small dream. 99

Victor Hugo

66 You see things and say, why? But I dream things that never were and say, why not? 99

George Bernard Shaw

66 Do not go where the path may lead; go instead where there is no path, and leave a trail. 99

Ralph Waldo Emerson, American philosopher

66 A hen is only an egg's way of making another egg. 99

Samuel Butler, English poet

66 No great discovery was made without a bold guess. 99

Isaac Newton

" The future belongs to those who believe in the beauty of their dreams. **"**

Eleanor Roosevelt

" Why not go out on a limb? Isn't that where the fruit is? **"**

Reader's Digest

" The real voyage of discovery consists not of seeing new landscapes, but of having new eyes. **"**

Marcel Proust

Having imagination and using it is an integral part of being a good manager, not an optional extra. But it needs development. It's no use waiting until a great idea comes around the corner and bites you on the leg. You have to look at a situation through new eyes, or step outside the box. The techniques of lateral thinking pioneered by Edward de Bono are a good example of this approach.

Look at the diagram below. Your task is to draw four lines through all nine points without lifting your pencil. If you stay literally inside the box, it's impossible – try it!

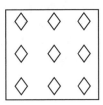

But try stepping outside the limits that we automatically put around the problem – the boundaries that artificially constrain our thinking – and see what becomes possible:

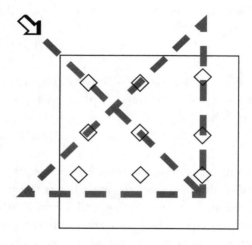

The best way to generate ideas depends on the people involved and the way they usually work together. For teams, brainstorming sessions, training programmes, away days and retreats can all produce useful results. For individual managers, using your imagination is an active process; it isn't just about keeping an open mind, which is passive. Good managers are creative in the way they look at situations and the way they identify actions to take. They are constantly using Kipling's "six honest men."

The Virtues for Managing Act Together as a Net

Using any of the virtues for managing will enable an individual to become a better manager. But an outstanding manager has to follow *all* the virtues. The good news is that one virtue often prompts you to consider others. For instance, good managers are results-oriented (virtue 14). On what results do they focus? – The results they need to meet their objectives (virtue 3).

As another example, consider what happens when good managers conclude they have more things to do than they have time for. What do they do? They delegate (virtue 7). And how do they know they can delegate? Because they have developed the people who work for them (virtue 9). And how do they know their people will do the work? Because they are good motivators (virtue 10). In fact, the individual virtues reinforce one another in the same way that individual threads intersect with others to create a net that can be used to catch a fish.

In the next chapter we look at some real-life situations and use the virtues for managing to identify a sound way to proceed. We can see how the virtues work together to enable managers to cope with the multitude of situations in which they find themselves.

Management virtues act together

03

The Virtues for Managing in Action

"What shall I do?" is a question managers throughout the world ask and answer day in, day out. To have any value, the virtues for managing have to be usable in the actual situations in which individual managers find themselves. In this chapter, we describe typical situations and show how the virtues can be used to find a way forward.

We noted down the thoughts that occurred to us as we considered how each virtue might be applied in each situation: for example, how to be a motivator in the context of trying to manage your boss. The last virtue, being imaginative, had a special role in this process, in that we tried to apply it in thinking about all the other virtues (using Kipling's six men -- What, Why, When, How, Where, and Who) rather than as a separate step of its own. In responding to the question "What shall I do?" we tried to develop a course of action that brought all the virtues into play – or at least wasn't inconsistent with any of the virtues.

We make no claim that our analyses and proposals

represent the only solutions, or even the best ones. But we are convinced that thinking about a situation from the viewpoint of each virtue in turn is an excellent way of analysing its managerial aspects, and can be used to generate sound responses to problems. We say "each virtue in turn" because omitting to apply one could easily lead to failure:

66 The chain is as strong as its weakest link. 99

Remember that your responses to one virtue will help generate responses to others: your priorities may derive from actions related to your objectives, or to the need to regain control, and so on. The power of the virtues lies partly in the way they reinforce one another.

We will now consider a series of cases borrowed from real life. Our aim is to show you how to apply the virtues in a range of situations so that you can address your own management problems as and when they arise.

Managing Your Boss

Let's begin with a difficult problem that no one likes to have to face – or has been trained to solve.

THE SITUATION

It's near the end of the day, and your boss asks you to come to his office. You've been dreading him asking you to do extra work just as he did yesterday and the day before that and the day before that. It's all too much. Your partner is fed up with you coming home late and exhausted. You hinted to your boss yesterday that enough was enough, but he obviously didn't get the message, because here he is asking you to write a report for tomorrow morning. You mutter that you'll do your best and beat a hasty retreat, complaining to your trusty secretary that it's a pity your boss doesn't know how to manage his team.

What are you going to do? You are fed up. How late will it be before you get home tonight? What are you going to say to your partner? Whatever you do, you are sure to upset someone: your boss, your partner or your staff.

USING THE VIRTUES TO FIND A SOLUTION

So how can you use the virtues to find a good solution to your predicament?

The process consists of five stages:

Make time to think what you are going to do as a manager in this situation.

Sit down with a sheet of paper to make notes on how you might respond.

Take each of the virtues in turn and think imaginatively about what it suggests you do (think? explore? plan?) This ensures your actions will be consistent with the virtues.

Write down your responses under each virtue.

Combine your separate responses into a coherent and logical set of actions that are individually and collectively consistent with the virtues.

Let's look at how this might work with your difficult boss, taking the virtues in order. We have written this section in the first person to mirror the kind of thoughts you might have in this situation, and we have added our own commentary in parentheses.

1. Having the courage to confront situations.

- ❏ Do I want this sort of thing to continue? No – I want it to stop as soon as possible. I'd better face up to the fact that I've got to do something about it. I need to confront my boss. How do I do this: face to face, in a letter, in an email, via a mediator?

(You recognise that the present situation is intolerable and unsustainable. The only way you can end it is by facing up to the boss and choosing the most appropriate action to take.)

2. Understanding my priorities.

- ❏ My first priority is to establish a reasonable dialogue with my boss.
- ❏ What are my work priorities? What are the low-priority tasks that could be postponed, passed on to someone else, or even dumped?
- ❏ What are my boss's priorities?
- ❏ What are the company's priorities? Quality, reputation and client service are far more important than short-term cash flow.

(You are beginning to identify your priorities, and moving on to identify low priorities that can be delegated or dispensed with. You are also using lateral thinking to consider others' priorities, which may be important in working out a win+win solution.)

3. Knowing my objectives.

- ❐ Do my boss and I agree on my work objectives?
- ❐ What are my objectives in this particular situation? To regain control of my work? To give my partner the time they deserve? To demonstrate my managerial skills to my team and the boss's boss?
- ❐ What are my boss's objectives? To browbeat me? To see how I react under pressure? To see how much slack there is in my department? Are these objectives legitimate, or sanctioned?

(You have articulated your objectives, and by thinking imaginatively you have also extended the virtue to the objectives of the others involved, in this case your boss. As before, this helps you fulfil the virtue of win+win.)

4. Listening and learning.

- ❐ Who should I talk to? The team? My old mentor? People who used to work for my boss? I will need time to do this.

(You have drawn up a list of people to talk to before you finalise your solution. You have also recognised that you

can't do this immediately, so you have to find time to
complete it, and to manage the process properly.)

5. Knowing myself.

- ☐ What are my strengths? Analysis, technical ability:
  how am I going to leverage them?
- ☐ And my weaknesses? I hate confrontation and find it
  hard to delegate: how am I going to overcome these?
- ☐ What about my boss's weaknesses and strengths?
  Not too sure about this – need to check out my
  first thoughts.

(You need to bear in mind the strengths you will draw
on in this situation, and the weaknesses you need to
avoid. Again, you are using this virtue imaginatively to
ask the same questions of your boss so as to develop a
win+win solution.)

6. Believing in teams.

- ☐ Appealing to the boss to treat me like a member
  of his team doesn't look a very promising strategy,
  but it may work for the boss's boss and head of
  personnel, so I'd best be seen as a team player.
- ☐ I need to involve the team in developing a solution.
  Does any of them have a similar problem? We will
  sink or swim together!

(Here, you are recognising that a manager belongs to a
number of teams and that it is necessary to consider the

members, purpose and tactics of each one.)

7. Believing in delegation.
- ☐ Have I delegated everything I can?
- ☐ Has the team delegated or outsourced everything it can?

(You've asked two important questions that need to be answered before you can come up with a firm solution. You can now see one possibility: to ask others to take on some of the tasks.)

8. Knowing the value of time.
- ☐ Have I cut out all unnecessary work?
- ☐ Am I spending time on unproductive activities?
- ☐ How much time do I want to spend working in the office, or at home, or on the train?

(There are no answers at this stage, but you are beginning to explore practical ways of finding more time to concentrate on what you can and should do.)

9. Believing in people development.
- ☐ I may need to do more training if we take on extra staff to deal with all this work. But will the recent increase in the workload continue, or is it just temporary?

(People development may not be a major factor in the

answer to this problem, but you shouldn't ignore it. If you can come up with a satisfactory solution, it will represent a significant act of self-development for you.)

10. Being a motivator.

❑ I can probably convince staff to put extra effort into increasing productivity, but I can't work people at full stretch all the time; we won't have any reserves for tackling a crisis. What kind of inducements or incentives would work?

(Here, you are using the virtue to generate yet another option for solving the problem, as well as identifying constraints.)

11. Being in control of the situation

❑ Obviously I'm not! I must develop a solution that puts my work and my life back into balance.

❑ How did I get caught out? How I am going to make sure it doesn't happen again?

❑ I must be in control from now on. I always need to have an achievable and agreed plan.

(Here you are using two virtues – knowing your objectives and identifying your priorities – in order to achieve a third: to gain control of the situation. You are also imaginatively looking backwards and forwards in time so that you can learn from your mistakes. Prevention is better than cure.)

12. Looking for win+win outcomes.

- ☐ I'll have to meet my boss's demands somehow, if he persists in them. Or I have to get him to recognise that the demands he is making are unreasonable.
- ☐ I need to be prepared to sell my solution to him so that it looks like *his* solution.
- ☐ Maybe I can propose that he helps me to develop myself to prevent future problems arising.
- ☐ Will he regard this situation as out of the ordinary and accept unusual responses, such as turning some of the work into special projects?

(You are recognising the power structure here: your proposed solution has to be feasible from your boss's point of view. But you have also realised that if your boss thinks in win+win terms, this may be something you can turn to your advantage.)

13. Taking decisions and sticking to them.

- ☐ I've got to be seen to take the final decision on what we do and when, even though the boss will have helped shape it. I mustn't ask him what to do or I'll look weak and get stuck in the same old rut because he will still be thinking that he makes all the decisions.

(You can achieve clarity in using the virtue of making decisions by applying the What, When, Where, Why,

How, Who tools: who could take what decisions? What is decided? and so on.)

14. Being results-oriented.

☐ After this difficulty, it will be vital to achieve required results in terms of quality as well as time for the sake of my and my team's future credibility.

☐ Should we move the targets slightly? Perhaps my boss will agree when he realises the costs that might be involved in meeting all his deadlines.

(Here, you acknowledge that a result has to be achieved and also identify another element of a possible solution.)

15. Being imaginative.

(There's nothing to add here because you will have been using Kipling's honest men as you went along thinking about each virtue. Now that you have reached the end of the list, perhaps you have more thoughts on how you can imaginatively apply the other virtues).

You now have all the elements of your solution. All you have to do is combine them to create a logical action plan. Remember that there are no correct answers. As the manager in this tricky situation, you are the only one who knows all the facts. You need to analyse the situation, decide what to do, and then *do it*.

To give you an example, here is what we would propose to do:

1. Go and tell my boss that I am working with my team on how we are going to do all the work we have to do in a timely and efficient manner. In other words, leave it with me and I'll take care of it. Remind the boss which work may suffer as a result.
   As well as putting me in charge, this also buys me time. When will I be able to tell him what the team proposes to do?

2. Work out my boss's real priorities. What would he think if we were to stretch some of the target dates on the jobs he has asked us to do? What are his constraints with his boss?

3. With my team, work out a normal work plan for doing the jobs based on our present levels of effort, resources and so on.

4. What is the time gap? How late will we be on which jobs? (Assuming that we have allocated the right priorities to different jobs.)

5. With the team, work out how the gap could be closed and what it would take:
   a. What resources do we have as a team? Can we tap them more effectively?

    b. Is it possible to improve our productivity and find a better, more efficient way of doing things?

    c. Should we stop doing some of the things we have traditionally done? What will happen if we do? Or can we transfer tasks to someone else? Or do them differently? Or delay them (if so, by how long)?

    d. Could we borrow some extra staff?

    e. Could we use temps?

    f. Could we recruit more staff?

6. Rank these options in terms of my boss's objectives, my team's objectives and finally my objectives. Bear in mind other relevant criteria such as impact and cost.

7. Agree with my team which option(s) come closest to a win+win outcome.

8. Design the presentation I will have to make to my boss. Ensure that it explains my plan fully and that it is acceptable to my boss.

9. Rehearse the presentation: what questions will the boss ask? What are our answers? (This ensures I will always be in control when we meet.)

10. Decide which member(s) of the team should come with me to the meeting. List the actions we have to take to implement the plan.

COMMENTARY

As we said earlier, a problem is just a list of things to do, and now we have a list that will solve the problem of managing your boss. Moreover, you haven't lost your temper in the process. In fact, you may be stronger because you have started to do things you probably ought to have been doing anyway, such as finding ways to increase your team's productivity. Maybe the boss was right to press you so hard – maybe that's his way of managing you. But now you have found a way to manage him.

Managing Your Team

THE SITUATION

When the time came for you to find a job, you joined the management training scheme at your local departmental store. You've been there ever since. You've made good progress, and you like the place. Since you were made store manager last year, you've derived a real sense of satisfaction from the way your team serves the local community. Staff turnover is very low, except among the shop assistants.

However, you are concerned about the bigger picture. Your store is no longer the brightest in the high street. That seems to be true of the other branches across the country, if you can judge by colleagues' remarks at the last managers' meeting. So it was no great surprise when the chairman of your company resigned and was replaced by someone much younger. The press claimed the big investors wanted new blood and had pushed him aside. You remember saying that this didn't seem fair after all the effort the old man had put in over the years.

Your new boss came to see you yesterday. It was only the second time you had met. She told you in confidence that the company was going to rationalise the product range and introduce new lines. There were to be new sales targets in terms of revenue per square foot, and she felt that staff at all levels would need to be reduced by at least 20% if profit targets were to be achieved. She wanted to know as soon as possible how you proposed to reduce your staff. She mentioned something about redundancy payments, but you were too shocked to take it in.

What are you going to do? What are you going to say when she comes to see you tomorrow?

FINDING A SOLUTION USING THE VIRTUES
1. Having the courage to confront situations.

☐ I have to talk to all my senior staff and managers as soon as I possibly can, before my boss arrives. They'll expect it. They know something's going on. Some of them will have talked to one another and put two and two together.

☐ I've also got to explain my own position. I've got to be realistic and state the facts, not succumb to speculation or gossip.

(You've recognised that you have to put the issues on the table so that you can continue to be in control. If you don't face your staff, you'll lose your credibility as well as their respect.)

2. Understanding my priorities.

- ☐ I need to handle all my staff honestly, and in a friendly manner.
- ☐ I need to be sensitive in handling those who have to go. I must find out how they will be selected and explain it to my staff.
- ☐ I must avoid a long period of indecision.
- ☐ I must identify ASAP the group of top staff who will stay, and work with them.

(You've compiled a clear and comprehensive statement of your priorities as a manager.)

3. Knowing my objectives.

- ☐ I can enhance my position as manager of the store by acting firmly but sympathetically.
- ☐ I can also put the future profitability of my store on a firmer footing.
- ☐ I need to coordinate – how much? – with the other branches. I don't want to be out of line.

(You've recorded your personal objective in handling the immediate issue of downsizing, as well as the most important objective for the store.)

4. Listening and learning.

- ☐ Who do I know who has been through this sort of thing before? I need to talk to them.
- ☐ I should listen to what the top staff group has to

say on who stays and who goes, and ensure that the criteria for selection stand up to scrutiny.

(You've recognized that you should do some research before taking any action.)

5. Knowing myself.
☐ I'm not sure how best to handle this. Must take advice!

(You've faced an uncomfortable fact about yourself and highlighted a weakness you need to address.)

6. Believing in teams.
☐ I need to work with the top staff group and think about how the team will operate in future.
☐ Can I get someone to come down from HQ to work directly with me or the top team? I certainly need to find out about our legal requirements and personnel policy.

(You've acknowledged that you have two teams to consider here: your own top staff, and your fellow store managers and support executives from HQ. Your more junior staff are also part of your team, but they aren't directly relevant to your present predicament.)

7 Believing in delegation.
☐ The top staff will have to participate in the

downsizing process by identifying who should
leave, and telling them.

(You've recognised that you are not the right person to
select the individuals or tell them.)

8. Knowing the value of time.
- ❐ This is an important issue that will affect the
  atmosphere of the whole store. I must give it
  50% of my time (two hours in the morning and
  two hours in the afternoon every day) until it is
  resolved.
- ❐ I must also make the timing of what I do
  consistent with that of other stores.

(You've understood that time is not just something
that you need to develop your way forward, but also
an essential aspect of co-ordinating your actions with
those of others.)

9. Believing in people development.
- ❐ Do we need training or counselling?
- ❐ Will some of the remaining staff need developing
  so that they can take on broader roles?
- ❐ Need to arrange retraining for staff who are going

(You've considered straightforward questions about both
the people remaining and those leaving your store.)

10 Being a motivator.
- ☐ My motivation is to make sure I stay and continue to progress.
- ☐ The same applies to the top staff group and so on down the line.
- ☐ For those going – a new opportunity?
- ☐ Stress the benefits of the plan to those staying.

(A number of different people will need to be motivated, and a problem for some may provide an opportunity for others.)

11. Being in control of the situation.
- ☐ I'll need a timed plan so that we can manage the process.
- ☐ I must explain the criteria for staying or going, and make sure that they are understood.

(You've recognised that the situation could easily get out of control without your close attention.)

12. Looking for win+win outcomes.
- ☐ Company wins if sales rise and costs fall; profits will go up too so long as customer service doesn't suffer.
- ☐ Some staff can win if they keep their jobs and get incentive payments.
- ☐ Even those who are leaving can win if we give them fair redundancy packages + retraining + help

with finding new jobs. Need to arrange for this
by contacting employment agencies etc. Why not
arrange some outplacement help for them? Should
we pay those whom we make redundant a bonus
next year based on the improvement in the store's
profits? After all, they have contributed to it, and
this would be one way of sharing the pain. Explain
this to them as soon as possible, even if I can't be
100% sure.

(Though the situation looks grim, you've applied this
virtue to find positive aspects for those who will suffer
the most.)

13. Taking decisions and sticking to them.
❒ If I don't bite this bullet, I'll be hit by the next.

(Deviating from the plan can lead only to disaster.)

14. Being results-oriented.
❒ Painful though this situation is, there are important
things I want to achieve:
❒ For the store: increasing its profitability.
❒ For the leavers: making sure a large percent are
retrained and find new jobs. Good plans are one
thing, but what will really count is my leadership
in arranging for the leavers to gain a new future.

(Overall objectives are almost always multi-faceted. Here they reflect both commercial and personal concerns.)

15. Being imaginative.

(You have been actively using this virtue as you thought about how to apply the other fourteen. But don't be afraid to think back over them and see what other possibilities you can come up with. You aren't likely to see the full impact of a virtue at the first attempt, as we found when we were writing this section. Often our thinking about one virtue would prompt ideas about another. For example, when we thought about how the situation could go out of control we realised it would be important to co-ordinate with the other branches, which then became an additional objective.)

So what is your answer? How are you going to manage this situation? Here's what we would suggest.

1. Find out about the redundancy package quickly; it was a big mistake not to have paid more attention. And contact HQ for some advice about handling redundancy, e.g. the kinds of question that people tend to ask.

2. Talk to all my top managers individually and confidentially about the need for change.

3. Arrange meeting tomorrow, before my boss comes,

to discuss criteria for deciding who should be made redundant. Identify unresolved issues such as who makes final decisions, dates and so on.

4. Agree actions with boss.

5. Tell those in the top group who will not be staying.

6. Contact local agencies for retraining courses, job-hunting advice, aptitude tests and so on.

7. Work with the top group to manage the downsizing process.

8. Refocus the minds of those who are staying on the future. What type of store will it be?

COMMENTARY
This story doesn't portray you as a good manager because (a) you are surprised at your boss's news and (b) the store is going downhill and apparently you are doing nothing about it. You need to regain management control.

Never let things take you by surprise; you'll have to think very quickly and sharply if you are to regain control.

Managing Your Key Investor
THE SITUATION
A few years ago, you were lucky enough to find a friend in need. But now your luck may be running out.

It all began when you became dissatisfied with your job at a big multinational. You'd had enough of working for someone else, and wanted the freedom to make your own decisions. You'd always been interested in cars and good at repairing them, and your wife suggested you do it for a living. Everything went well for a while: you recruited a few people and bought a garage with a steady fuel trade and expanding car sales. You were proud to be a successful small businessman, even if much of the garage belonged to the bank.

But then the recession came and life became much more difficult. Customers were taking longer to pay, yet suppliers were pushing you to settle your bills within 30 days. Interest rates went up, and so did your repayments to the bank. You feared you were going to go under. Then, out of the blue, one of your valued customers, a man named John, said something about the difficulties of financing this sort of business, and ended up making a major investment in your garage.

In fact, John now controls it. You get a regular salary, which takes care of your bills, but unfortunately John is so rich that he doesn't take the business seriously. You work on cars for him and his family and friends, but you have to be careful about chasing them for payment. When you added it all up recently, the money they owe you came to quite a large sum; no wonder your profit-sharing bonus didn't amount to much. The story is different when it comes to other customers, where John tells you to be much more hard-nosed – not at all the way you are used to operating.

You are getting more and more frustrated – but what can you do?

USING THE VIRTUES TO FIND A SOLUTION

In the previous two case studies we provided commentaries to help you understand the thinking behind the notes on each virtue. We hope you found them useful. But now, to develop your understanding of how to apply the virtues, we are going to leave it to you to work out how to interpret the notes we have made.

1. Having the courage to confront situations.

☐ If I hide my head in the sand, I'll continue to feel frustrated and the business will go downhill. This will reflect very badly on me. I need to find the courage to have a meeting with John to explore a way forward that I can agree to, not have imposed on me.

2. Understanding my priorities.

☐ My first priority is to identify realistic options for me to continue in the business.

☐ What are John's priorities? They don't appear to include the business.

☐ I need to devote some time to finding out.

3. Knowing my objectives.

☐ My objectives: reasonable regular income; interesting job; status in peer group.

❐ John's objectives: status; to ingratiate himself with friends; not to lose money.

4. Listening and learning.
❐ Who should I talk to?
- Bank manager? Probably not.
- My accountant? Maybe.
- Owner's business partner? No.
- My wife? Who else?

❐ John should listen more carefully about the business, and not just the financial aspects. I must make time to sit down with him and get him to understand.

5. Knowing myself.
❐ My strengths: knowledge of the technology and engineering; fanatical about quality; trusted, enthusiastic, good at doing deals and networking.
❐ My weaknesses: business processes, finance, interpersonal effectiveness? Delegation? Am I getting bored?

6. Believing in teams.
❐ Maybe I haven't involved John enough in the business. We started off with him as the financier and me as the technician, but maybe that's a divisive approach. How can we form an enthusiastic business-oriented team rather than a dry, formal financial management team?

7. Believing in delegation.

☐ Could I delegate more of the day-to-day management of the business and do other things instead, such as spending time with potential customers at car events? Or spend more time working with John?

8. Knowing the value of time.

☐ I've got this wrong recently; I've spent too much time brooding in vain over the situation.

☐ And maybe I spend too much time fixing cars and not enough on resolving people issues.

☐ I could do with spending more time at home too.

9. Believing in people development.

☐ If I delegate more, which of my staff will need training up to be a supervisor or a workshop manager? How long will this take?

10. Being a motivator.

☐ Who do I have to motivate? Mainly John – and then the prospective supervisors and manager.

11. Being in control of the situation.

☐ I'm not in control at the moment. I get swept along by the day-to-day activities of the business. I need to draw up a plan to change things. If I managed my time better in the business, I could spend more time with John or do other things such

as assess how the staff members' skills could be
better used.

12. Looking for win+win outcomes.

- ☐ If I do more things outside of the business, what's
  in it for John? Why should he agree?
- ☐ He needs to keep me because my name and
  reputation count for something, I think. But I
  won't go on working for ever; the time will come
  when I need to retire. Maybe I need to recruit
  someone else to work with me and eventually take
  over. If they are younger and cheaper, that will
  keep John happy.
- ☐ I wonder how long John himself intends to stay in
  the business.
- ☐ Are there any other ways that I can win while John
  wins too?

13. Taking decisions and sticking to them.

- ☐ What are my realistic options: leave, go part-time,
  reorganise?
- ☐ What would John do if he knew I was unhappy:
  replace me, help me?

14. Being results-oriented.

- ☐ I still need a good income (those astronomical
  school fees), so I have to make sure that whatever
  I do, I protect it. If the worst comes to the worst I
  shall have to stick it out. No, that's defeatist.

❏ I must have courage and make things change, or
my situation can only get worse.

15. Being imaginative.

(As before, you may want to review the way you have
approached the virtues and see if you could add to it.).

So what is the answer – how are you going to manage
this situation?

Here are our thoughts.

Strategy

I must involve John in the solution, which means involving
him more in the business – *all* the business. So I must make
more time for him and demand more time from him. To
do that, I must delegate more, so I'd better start by finding
good supervisors.

Actions

1   Tell John that I want a meeting to talk about our
strategy. I'm getting on in years; we need to think
about the future and look at the big picture. I'll need
to plan carefully for the meeting.

2   Hold the meeting. Take John out to lunch, away from
office and telephone, mobiles off. Tell him we need to
ensure the long-term sustainability of the business and
there are important issues we need to discuss. Tell him
he can still achieve his aims.

3. Agree staff structure (e.g. forecourt manager, workshop manager, administration manager) and people best suited to the jobs. Draw up outline job descriptions. To be credible, we need to have weekly management meetings rather than monthly directors' meetings. Crucial that John attends. We also need agreed annual plans and budgets, and sound financial procedures. As CEO, I and not John should work with the accountant to develop them.

4 Identify the new managers' development needs and arrange training; keep an eye on the cost.

5. I must delegate more. I should have a regular slot in the management meeting agenda to discuss things I haven't delegated. Must pose the question as "How I can involve someone else?" rather than starting from the implicit assumption that only I can do it.

6. Reduce the number of hours I work. Get my secretary to keep a diary and weekly totals. Refocus my working hours on genuine priorities, not the things that are urgent.

COMMENTARY

Here you have evaluated your investor's aims in terms of your own, helping you to develop a viable solution. Long-term thinking is always important. Where do you want to end up? If that isn't at the end of the path you are on now, you are on the wrong path.

Note that the solution here is a series of interlocking actions. Several areas need attention: some are to do with you, some with the business, and some with John. So the right approach is to act on a number of things that together address all the issues. A common mistake is to expect one action to solve many issues. It seldom does. This is deeply frustrating, because you have done something constructive and yet the situation you find yourself in has not improved. Just remember:

> **❝**You need to repair all the holes in the bucket to stop the water running out.**❞**

Starting Your Own Business[8]
THE SITUATION
Over the past few years, John and Jennifer Williams have become increasingly involved in producing and packaging toffee. Back in the 1950s, John's father made toffee to his own special recipe that was a big hit with everyone who tried it. After he died, John's mother produced small batches of the toffee for family, friends and neighbours in her village. Both the cooking and the contact with people meant a lot to her. Gradually, John became involved too, helping his mother out with what was developing into a small family business.

After his mother died, John kept up the tradition. He and his wife Jennifer were persuaded to run a stall at the local village fete. The sales exceeded their wildest dreams, but building up enough stock took a great deal of work. As the assistant manager of a local high street bank, John works long hours in his day job, and is also expected to be active in community bodies such as the Rotary Club. Jennifer is busy at home looking after two young children and singing in the church choir, but both of them make time to run the toffee business on the side.

The first year was fun, but by the second year things were beginning to get out of hand. The Williamses are enthusiastic people who never do things by halves, but now virtually all their spare time is spent on toffee. John has begun to wonder whether his future should be in banking – which has changed considerably in recent years, and no one's job is secure any more – or in confectionery, or indeed in something else entirely.

He decides that tonight, after Jennifer has gone to choir practice and he has put the children to bed, he will use the virtues of managing to plan out what he is going to do.

USING THE VIRTUES TO FIND A SOLUTION
This is what we wrote when we applied the virtues to the situation John faces.

1. Having the courage to confront situations.
- ☐ We can't carry on as we are. We have no time to ourselves. It's all work, kids and toffee.
- ☐ I shall either have to tell the boss I am leaving or agree with Jennifer that the toffee has to revert to a sideline.
- ☐ I had better set myself a deadline: say, three or four weeks.

❏ If I go ahead with toffee, what will be the major challenges I need the courage to overcome: sales effort, money, getting people to help, motivating them to succeed?

2. Understanding my priorities.

❏ I need an income (the mortgage, the school fees, holidays, living costs...).

❏ I want time to enjoy myself with the family.

❏ But then I want my job to be a challenge as well as worth while. At the bank, the only challenge I've faced in recent months has been to cope with new systems and regulatory control – not exactly stimulating.

❏ Should I stick to toffee: yes or no?

❏ Cash will be king.

3. Knowing my objectives.

❏ Must ensure that the children have a full family life; the worst thing would be to fail as a parent. That means giving them time and money and being a good role model.

❏ I'd like to retire while I am still fairly young and not have my job dominate my whole life.

❏ If I choose to make toffee, my objective will be to make and sell large quantities of the stuff. But what about supplies, mass-production logistics, quality, premises, sales force, distributors?

4. Listening and learning.

- ☐ When I had my last career review, the bank made it clear I was regarded as a solid individual – a good chap to guide the rising stars who are passing through, but not one of them.
- ☐ I need to have a serious talk with one of the new Rotary members. Tom used to work in the City but now sells smart dresses in the high street with his wife.
- ☐ Who else can help me with advice? Any chance of government funding? They are always talking about helping small firms. But I'd better be careful about who I talk to – I don't want my plans to get back to the bank.

5. Knowing myself.

- ☐ I don't mind working hard, so that doesn't worry me.
- ☐ But what about the uncertainty if I opt for toffee? We aren't used to taking risks; everything has always been cut and dried before. Better try to identify the risks and prepare for them.
- ☐ We've put some money aside for a rainy day. What would happen if we invested it in toffee, and everything came unstuck?
- ☐ Do I have an aptitude for toffee making? Or am I just following in my father's footsteps – something I probably haven't acknowledged in my life? Is that enough to make a success of it? How can I improve my know-how?
- ☐ Can I organise the selling side effectively?

6. Believing in teams.

- ☐ Even if Jennifer comes to work in the toffee business full time, we couldn't produce enough week by week to generate a reasonable income. We would need a team. Who? How many? Where from?
- ☐ Could we franchise the idea somehow? Who knows about franchising? I remember seeing a book on it a few years ago; must ring head office and borrow a copy.
- ☐ We might also need help around the house and someone to do the school run, especially when the kids are doing after-school activities.

7. Believing in delegation.

- ☐ We can delegate some of the work, especially on the administration side, although that's what I am good at.
- ☐ Could we get other people interested in toffee making, especially younger ones? Then I could look after marketing and admin.
- ☐ But we won't delegate bringing up our children.

8. Knowing the value of time.

- ☐ If I take the toffee route, how will I make enough profit without spending too much time? I need to do some careful planning.
- ☐ Actually, I need some time *now* to analyse the

options. Can't do that on the bus going to work. Maybe we could begin trying to get some help – a sort of experimental start-up of the business? That could buy me some time.

9. Believing in people development.

❏ I suppose I could save money by employing young people at low wages and teaching them how to make toffee so I that can delegate. But how long would it take me, and what would I have to give up to make time for training? Will the trainees value what I teach them? Remember, training is an investment.

❏ Perhaps I could find suitable staff via local vocational training courses. Who would I contact about this?

10. Being a motivator.

❏ What will be my motivation in pursuing toffee making? Independence? Higher family income? Fame? Doing something my father wanted to do?

❏ What will motivate Jennifer? Her love for me? Is that fair? What does *she* want to do?

❏ Why should anyone want to join me? Just to have a job? A romantic soul who likes the idea of preserving the art of toffee-making? Someone keen on belonging to a small business?

11. Being in control of the situation.

- ☐ If I decide to stay at the bank, how long will they want to keep me? Will I be retired early? I'd like to have a contingency plan in mind. Can I ask for redundancy now? A lump sum would be very helpful. I must check my pension as well.

- ☐ I need a production plan, a sales plan and a financial plan for the toffee business. Not sure what money we make now from our hobby – something, certainly, but how much per hour we work? What is our break-even point for sales? Is it realistically achievable? Can I maintain the flavour at higher production volumes? When will I need extra premises?

- ☐ What about food regulations? We've managed to disregard them so far because everything has been unofficial.

12. Looking for win+win outcomes.

- ☐ Leaving the bank might be a win for me, but only if I choose the right job. Not convinced yet that toffee making will be a win.

- ☐ What else could I do? What am I good at: numbers, mathematics, business matters? On the radio tonight the government announced special incentives to attract maths teachers. Am I qualified? Probably not.

- ☐ What about administrative work? In schools, or maybe in the health sector? These would provide more certain futures than toffee making, but only

in the short term; in the longer term I might be
made redundant, and then I might have trouble
finding another job.

13. Taking decisions and sticking to them.

☐ What are my options? Staying at the bank?
Toffee making? Education? Not book-keeper,
nor accounting. Financial adviser? Maybe. My
background would go down well: not so much a
hard sell but making a sale on my probity. Maybe
a transfer within the bank? That's an interesting
idea, but would it happen? Probably not. Would
the long-term security be any greater? No – so not
such a good idea after all.

☐ When do I need to decide?

14. Being results-oriented.

☐ I need to resolve this situation. I'll have to do more
thinking, but I'd better not take too long, or I may
fail to meet any of my objectives.

15. Being imaginative

☐ Have I thought of everything?

So how should John manage the situation? This is our
analysis.

He concludes:

☐ Toffee making or staying with the bank are my
only realistic options at present.

❏ Clearly I'm not totally convinced about the toffee idea yet. But the more I think about it, the more reservations I have about staying with the bank.

❏ If we can make the toffee option a success, that will be the best for us.

So what do I need to do to make toffee a success? Let me use the virtues again:

Courage: Address all the challenges I face – don't shirk.
Priorities:
1. Market research to assess possible sales levels at given price/quality levels
2. Estimate production costs: materials and labour
3. Assess peak funding requirement and possible sources
4. Identify potential production workers, even if I have to train them
5. Maintain our reputation for quality handmade toffee, which means focusing on suppliers and total quality management.

Objectives: Generate a reasonable monthly income for me and Jennifer within six months. Earn an acceptable return on the funds invested in the business.
Listening and learning: Meet Tom from Rotary and his wife.
Knowing myself: Need to have my toffee-making skills checked out. Must be sure they are good enough to sustain a commercial operation.

Teams: Contact local colleges for possible staff. Find out about franchising.

Delegation: Ask Jennifer if she will try and find suitable staff.

Time: Complete initial feasibility study within four weeks. Take two weeks' leave from bank to make this possible.

People development: Ask Jennifer to identify any toffee-making training courses or sources of expertise.

Motivator: Develop suitable incentive systems for production staff and sales people, and possible franchisees. Shares in the business?

In control: Need sales plan, production plan and annual budget. Need simple recording systems to produce monthly management reports on performance.

Have monthly review meetings to assess progress.

Win+win: Look for a collaborator or associate organisation if that will reduce risk.

Takes decisions / Results oriented: If my feasibility study indicates there's a good chance of meeting my objectives, then I will go for it.

Imaginative: Is there anything I've overlooked?

COMMENTARY

Although John's conclusions are unremarkable, this example demonstrates the power of using the virtues. They help to expose your real thoughts about all the relevant factors in deciding what to do both immediately and three or four weeks later, when you are ready to make a definite decision.[9]

Handling an Untruthful Member of Staff[10]

THE SITUATION

At a Christmas party, you happen to meet a man who claims to know one of your sales staff, a man named Greg. After testifying to Greg's success at winning big sales bonuses, as well as his popularity with women, he shocks you by saying that Greg spent six months in jail after being convicted of grievous bodily harm for assaulting his wife. Back at work, you look into the allegation and find that Greg didn't mention his conviction on his application form or during his interviews. When you challenge him, he admits that he didn't tell the whole truth, but explains that when he was open about his past in previous job applications, he was rejected out of hand.

Not only is Greg the best salesman in your division, he is the best in the company. He is a top performer, and very popular with his colleagues and his customers. In fact, personnel have put him on their list of future top managers. What do you do now?

USING THE VIRTUES TO FIND A SOLUTION

Let's look at how you might think through the problem using the virtues as a prompt.

1. Having the courage to confront situations.

- ☐ Either Greg is lying or he has failed to divulge information he was asked to supply. The rules are clear. Both are dismissible offences.
- ☐ Honesty is vital. It's an integral part of our ethical business policy.

❏ Hard though it may be, we can't have different rules for different people.

2. Understanding my priorities.

❏ I'll be understanding and sympathetic, but I must tell personnel.

❏ I need to be seen to be fair to everyone: colleagues, customers and suppliers as well as Greg.

❏ I'll try and help him by explaining the situation clearly.

3. Knowing my objectives.

❏ Greg has to leave.

❏ I could help him find a new job, or at least give him time to do so, possibly via a paid leave of absence?

❏ I must tell Greg that the references we give will be accurate and fair to all concerned.

4. Listening and learning.

❏ Check with personnel on company policy, any precedents, and leave of absence issue.

❏ Ask about any help for offenders in re-establishing their lives, especially any support groups.

5. Knowing myself.

❏ I will feel uncomfortable doing this, so I must rehearse and stay calm.

❏ I have some sympathy with his predicament, but

not with his deception. Honesty is the best policy? No, it's the only policy.

6. Believing in teams.

- ☐ Confirm my decision and approach with the rest of the management team: the boss, head of personnel, and head of marketing. We must all take the same view. Their support will give me confidence.

7. Believing in delegation.

- ☐ Delegate what? Support/counselling for Greg? Is there a specialist outplacement group that could help? I doubt it's the first time this has happened.
- ☐ Delegate some tasks to give me time to prepare for my meeting with Greg.

8. Knowing the value of time.

- ☐ Find an appropriate time to meet Greg; mid-afternoon might be best. Rearrange diary to make sure this is possible.
- ☐ Now we know, we need to move quickly to dispel the uncertainty. It's better for Greg to know where he stands.

9. Believing in people development.

- ☐ We should offer Greg counselling so that he can face up to the loss of his job and find a new one.
- ☐ We need to help him deal with his past.

10. Being a motivator.

- ❏ How have others with a criminal record found work? I saw something about this in the newspapers last week – I need to find the article.
- ❏ We must show Greg that honesty is vital, however difficult it may be.
- ❏ Explain that we are all hurt by this situation: he is losing his job and we are losing a good salesman.

11. Being in control of the situation.

- ❏ Check whether the company policy has been reviewed recently. What do other companies do? I should check what course of action is recommended by the CBI and other business organisations.
- ❏ People will be sympathetic to Greg; we'll need to tell them the reasons for his departure as soon as possible after he leaves. We'll need to agree what each of us will say.
- ❏ We will need to give his customers a truthful explanation and their new sales contact.

12. Looking for win+win outcomes.

- ❏ Get Greg to see what he did wasn't right. We'll do what we can to help him find a new job.
- ❏ Greg's departure will give us an opportunity to make improvements in the structure and staffing of the sales department. We must explain the benefits of this to customers.

13. Taking decisions and sticking to them.
- ❑ He has to go. I must tell him tomorrow.

14. Being results-oriented.
- ❑ We need to replace Greg as soon as possible. He was a terrific salesman and his customers were key.
- ❑ If we don't move quickly, we may miss our sales targets.

15. Being imaginative.
- ❑ I'll just run through all the other virtues to see if there is anything I can add.

So what are you going to do? Here's what your plan of action might look like:

- ❑ Talk to personnel as soon as possible. In addition, recommend that all recruits be checked via the Criminal Records Bureau.
- ❑ Talk to boss tomorrow, around midday if possible.
- ❑ Rehearse meeting with Greg, then talk to him tomorrow afternoon.
  - • Be firm
  - • Be sympathetic
  - • Be helpful and hopeful
  - • Be grateful for his work and contribution
  - • Stay calm.
- ❑ Brief the sales managers the following morning. Let them tell individuals. No need to blow it up by having divisional management meeting.

❏   Arrange for Greg's customers to be contacted as a priority.

COMMENTARY

It would be easy to keep things brief and just say "Sorry, but those are the rules," or to leave personnel to deal with this as a disciplinary matter and simply add a few words of farewell at the end. However, this example shows how you can be a better manager by using the virtues to help you discharge your full responsibilities towards one of your staff within the constraints of your company's policies.

Handling Uncooperative Staff[11]
THE SITUATION

Janet has been appointed by a large national company to take charge of the management accounting department in one of its factories. The factory has been manufacturing a product that is nearing the end of its life cycle. Profits have been falling, and the outgoing manager has been tightening capital budgets and raising performance targets to cut costs. A new product is gradually being brought into production, and one of Janet's first tasks is to introduce small changes in data collection and processing associated with controlling the costs of the new product.

The trouble is, any changes Janet asks for are met by groans and grumbles from her staff: "That's not the sort of work I am supposed to do." "I don't know how to do this – I haven't been trained for it." "I've got far too much to do already." "Mike has hardly anything to do; give it to him."

"Sarah is the expert on this; she'll find it easy."

Janet can see that many of these claims simply aren't true. Some staff are sitting around pretending to be busy even though they have completed their immediate tasks; others resent having to stay late to finish jobs off. Janet finds she can't rely on her people to pass messages on, and they are unhelpful to each other too. However much they may try to ingratiate themselves with her, they are reluctant to try out new systems even if they are patently better than the current software.

What should Janet do?

USING THE VIRTUES TO FIND A SOLUTION

Here are Janet's thoughts about the virtues.

1. Having the courage to confront situations.

- ❏ This is totally unacceptable. I need to get to grips with my new staff and face them with the facts.

2. Understanding my priorities.

- ❏ There's a lot to do here. I need to determine new roles and responsibilities for my staff. I need to provide new motivations for them. I need to build them into a team.
- ❏ What is the optimum size for my group? I may need to reduce staff numbers or expand them.

3. Knowing my objectives.

- ❏ My objectives are to provide cost-effective

management information on time, and to keep the
group working together

☐ What are the objectives of my staff?

4. Listening and learning.

☐ I can hear what they are saying *now*, but what
were they saying before I arrived? Were they
badly managed? How were the departmental
performance targets introduced? Must find out,
but who to ask: the staff, the finance director, the
personnel department?

☐ I don't know my staff yet. I should talk to them
individually and get to know them and their
interests.

5. Knowing myself.

☐ This isn't my usual cup of tea; I am noted as a
technical expert. Ask Bill, my old mentor.

☐ Must avoid letting this situation drift, as I am
inclined to do.

☐ I'm not a natural team leader.

6. Believing in teams.

☐ There isn't any teamwork here. I should use the
word "team" only when we are talking positively
about the future. I don't want to find that I have
welded my staff into a team that is opposed to me.

☐ I must emphasise the interdependence of our
tasks and the way it affects our results. They aren't

working for me as their boss, but as a team aiming to succeed together.

7. Believing in delegation.

☐ I need to try and make everyone responsible for something, not just ask them to do things. Perhaps I should reorganise their work.

8. Knowing the value of time.

☐ I'll need to make sure I have enough time – say two weeks – to find a good solution before beginning implementation. I'd better reschedule my meeting with auditors about the next audit; it's not a priority just now.

☐ I must arrange individual meetings with staff, maybe one a day. That will give me time to reflect on them without the process dragging on for too long. But I don't want to rush it and make it appear that I'm just going through the motions.

9. Believing in people development.

☐ This could be the key to motivating my staff, but I need to identify what they need and what they want.

☐ Talk to personnel about any plans they may have for training and career development. The staff may well know more than I do about what is in the pipeline.

☐ Study last year's appraisals. Who should be trained, in what?

10. Being a motivator.

- ❐ What makes them tick? Do they all have different motives?
- ❐ Are they afraid of losing their jobs? Or are they so bored that they are pinning their hopes on redundancy payments? Or do they doubt the future of the company? Must find out how they see the situation.
- ❐ I'll need to hold a team meeting to get them to decide a way forward and become more committed.

11. Being in control of the situation.

- ❐ I'm not, and I need to be!
- ❐ I'll have to monitor my progress in improving the position. What targets do I need to set to do this?

12. Looking for win+win outcomes.

- ❐ Once I've found out what they want out of working at this company and out of their own careers, I need to align it to what I want them to do so that their work matches what they are looking for.

13. Taking decisions and sticking to them.

- ❐ They'll have to fall into line sooner or later, or they'll have to go. That may not be a good way of motivating them, but the alternative isn't a good way to run a business. Maybe one sacking might encourage the others.

14. Being results-oriented.
☐ I must set out their work programme in such a way that they will agree on targets and accept the consequences of good or bad performance.

15. Being imaginative.
☐ I think I've covered all the possibilities – but let me check.

So what are you going to do?

Here's what Janet decides.

☐ Do some digging on what happened under the old boss.

☐ Make the director of finance aware of the problem and my plans to resolve it, and get his co-operation.

☐ Make sure there is a clean break from the past. Actions speak louder than words.

☐ Talk to the staff individually.
- Listen to their problems. Empathise with them as far as possible.
- Tell them about my objectives, targets and departmental budget, plus company plans and progress.
- Mention future opportunities for good performers. Stress the importance that the top bosses place on high-quality information for managing the business. Get the finance director to support this view, but later on, and independently from me.

- Find out what they feel they can contribute, or not contribute.
- ☐ Hold a team meeting.
- On the basis of the results of the individual meetings, discuss the pros and cons of alternative ways of proceeding to meet our departmental objectives.
- Try and get them to develop the solution we adopt. If necessary, accept slightly inferior answer, but with agreement to monitor and redefine if outcomes fail to fulfil agreed criteria.
- The meeting has to end with each individual agreeing to a clear way forward, yardsticks for monitoring and a set of personal responsibilities.
- ☐ Report back to finance director that I have matters under control.
- ☐ Monitor everyone's performance, individually and as a team. Hold forward-looking team meetings. Encourage debate and self-management. Don't use the meetings to wield a stick.
- ☐ Formally appraise the individuals and the team. Give feedback in due course. Perhaps do 360-degree feedback?[12]

COMMENTARY

Janet decides she has to take a gradual step-by-step approach to gaining the support of her staff. It is seldom, if ever, possible to achieve all the virtues in one fell swoop. Implementing each one takes time.

This example illustrates how one virtue – being in control – can be pursued by using others, such as being a motivator and seeking win+win solutions. As we said earlier, our virtues are mutually supportive.

Conclusions

For us, the most interesting conclusion we have drawn from examining these difficult management situations is that none of the solutions have turned out to be complicated. They were all developed from straightforward answers as to how we could use each of our virtues in specific circumstances. They all involved a series of simple actions such as talking to someone, being clear about one's real aim(s), finding out about something, and so on. None of these actions should have involved sleepless nights or any other forms of stress. All we have done is take the answers to how we can use the individual virtues and assemble them into a logical and effective series of linked steps.

These cases show that our virtues can be used in practice to attack real problems and generate successful solutions. We challenge you to find a managerial problem where they can't be used to find a credible solution.

However, two questions remain unanswered. First, why do many people find it difficult to develop an effective series of simple steps to tackle managerial problems? And second, how can we learn to be a great manager by using our virtues at work? We consider both these questions in the next chapter.

What Next?

There are several reasons why people find it difficult to identify credible solutions to the problems they face as managers. One reason is that they don't have an underlying set of principles to which they can refer. We discussed this in chapter 1, when we explained why we set out on our journey to discover the virtues that underpin the actions of all great managers.

The other reason lies in the attitudes that some people bring to being a manager. They need to abandon them, and start using the virtues for managing.

Leaving the Wrong Attitudes Behind

Let us look first at some of the attitudes people bring to solving the managerial problems they face.

Some people jump straight to the answer. They are impatient or arrogant and think they know the answer. In their haste, they don't give themselves the time to find the right solution. It isn't easy to find good answers that are also simple, clear and readily understood, especially in tricky situations. Give yourself time to find the right answer. There is almost always time to think before you jump in. The aim is to find the right solution to the problem, rather than to give an answer within an arbitrary time frame. Remember the virtue of knowing your objectives.

A related problem is that sometimes **we are lazy** when we come to considering problems of managing. Not only do we not always devote sufficient time to solving problems, we may also not bother to think about the current problem and simply base our actions on what worked last time. This may work, but it is risky unless we check whether there are any significant differences between the situation then and now.

It is, of course, natural to **do things that we like** because we know we are good at doing them and feel comfortable doing them. But the solution that comes naturally may not be the most appropriate thing to do. Habit is the enemy of creativity.

We are all products of **our past experiences**. They are important, but generally only part of the way forward. They are at best signposts to solutions; at worst they create a false sense of calm before the storm that will surely follow.

Another fault is that many people are **blinkered in their thinking**. They don't let their mind wander far and wide to ensure they have considered all aspects. They provide a partial solution that doesn't deal with all of the issues involved. To counter this tendency, let your fantasies unwind!

Many people **focus on the next step** to be taken. This is wrong: we need to be thinking about the situation we want to bring about. Or to put it another way, we need to describe for ourselves a vision of what the situation will be after the problem has been satisfactorily resolved. Then we can work backwards to identify the steps we need to take in order to bring about our vision, using the virtues as our guide. Once you know where you are going, it is easy to take the individual steps.

None of us is without **prejudices**. We need to be aware of them and act to counter them when necessary.

Similarly, we may not think correctly about a situation: our **logic may be faulty** or we may **fail to recognise** some important piece of evidence.

> 66 We had the experience but missed the meaning 99
>
> *T. S. Eliot*

Clearly, none of these attitudes should form part of a manager's professional kitbag. If you recognise them in yourself, you will need to purge yourself of them.

So how do you do that?

What next?

Managing Yourself to Improve Yourself

It is tempting to write that improving yourself is simply another kind of management problem – a problem you have in managing yourself. In fact, it is so tempting that the only way we can honestly tackle this topic is to go through the virtues for managing and see where they lead us – and, more importantly, what they suggest you should do.

1. Having the courage to confront situations.

First, you need to recognise that you have a problem. You need to find the courage to try and do things differently even though people may comment on it, perhaps behind your back. Have the courage to ask people openly about your managerial qualities and how you might improve.

2. Understanding my priorities.

What are your worst weaknesses? What are the easiest to put right in terms of time, effort and courage? What will be your first step on the road to improvement?

3. Knowing my objectives.

When and how do you want to be a better manager? Remember to be realistic.

4. Listening and learning.

Do you observe others and analyse their performance? Try assessing how well they use the virtues. Where are they going wrong? How would you do it differently using the virtues? Talk to them – and listen.

5. Knowing myself.

How do you perform on each of the virtues? Make an honest evaluation of yourself; you can use the Self-Assessment Form in the appendix. Analyse how you perform in each managerial situation as you deal with it. What virtues did you use effectively, and which did you not? Making this assessment is important because it is difficult to know which way to go unless you know where you are starting from.[13]

6. Believing in teams.

Are there others in your group who also want to improve their performance as managers? Can you work together, for example, to discuss how to cope with situations you are both aware of? Who are the best managers in your peer group, and why?

7. Believing in delegation.

Can you delegate some of the difficult situations by asking others to resolve them? Do you become too involved in matters you don't need to handle yourself? But remember you can't delegate responsibility.

8. Knowing the value of time.

Deliberately set aside some time every day to analyse your performance. Use your journey time on the train going home, or perhaps when you are in the bath. Take enough time to use the virtues to work out what to do – but don't take *too* long.

9. Believing in people development.

Believe in developing yourself! All training requires practice, so practise in your mind (or on paper) how you would use each virtue in the kind of situation you find yourself in.

10. Being a motivator.

You are going to motivate yourself to follow the virtues for managing, so think what motivates you. Less stress? Better results? Better relationships with others because you won't upset people or disappoint them?

11. Being in control of the situation.

Try to identify difficult situations you have found yourself in, and plan how you will tackle them in the future. What are the fundamental elements of these situations? Make sure you have the virtues at your fingertips whenever you need them. Why not write them on a card and use it as a bookmark in your diary? Then you can refer to it when you are sitting at your desk, or in a meeting. Ask friends to let you know from time to time how well you are doing at improving as a manager.

12. Looking for win+win outcomes.

Identify who tends to suffer when your poor management causes problems for others. Getting them to help you with your programme will be a win+win for you both.

13. Taking decisions and sticking to them.

Be positive about changing yourself. Make it a rule to review *all* the virtues quickly to make sure you have taken them into account in your decision. If not, make a point of saying something like, "Yes, that's all very well, but what about … ?," or, "This may be a premature response; we need to think a bit more widely on this so that we don't jump the wrong way," or "I need some more time before I reach a firm decision."

14. Being results-oriented.

Take the time to review your performance every other month, say, until you are happy with it. And then keep reassessing yourself regularly, but perhaps less frequently.

15. Being imaginative.

You won't go far wrong if you always use Kipling's honest serving-men: What? Why? When? How? Where? Who?

Finally, remember this sporting adage to give you the determination to keep honing your use of the virtues:

66 Amateurs practise until they get it right. Professionals practise until they never make mistakes. 99

Let that be a guiding light for all great managers.

Simply a **GREAT** Manager

Notes

1 Angelo Dundee, quoted in *The King of the World*, Picador, London (1998), p. 92.

2 Joe Martin talking about Cassius Clay whom he introduced to boxing, quoted in *The King of the World*.

3 So You Think You're Mad: Seven practical steps to mental health. Paul Hewitt, Handsell, Gloucester (2001).

4 This came to one of us after listening to a sermon at Ampleforth College. It is easy to say we want to be good, but to be good we have to say no to bad things, otherwise we tend to carry on doing the wrong things without thinking. The bad things just seem to happen.

5 Note we did not write "work for them," which would not be consistent with the virtue of believing in teamwork.

6 He may have been paraphrasing Thomas Jefferson, who said: "I believe in luck and I find the harder I work the more I have of it."

7 Many people write "win–win", but we think a plus sign is more appropriate than a rule or a hyphen, which look like minus signs and so convey entirely the wrong impression.

[8] This is based on "John Williams, Entrepreneur," a case written by Roy McLarty, Suffolk Marketing Management Development Centre, distributed by the European Case Clearing House, Cranfield University.

[9] *The Times* of 24 October 2004 reported that a couple who had quit their banking jobs eight years earlier to make ice-cream had raised more than £1 million from investors in their company. Their own stake was valued at £1.6 million.

[10] This is based on an examination question from the Chartered Institute of Purchasing and Supply, quoted in *Principles of Management* by Tony Morden, McGraw-Hill, Maidenhead (1996).

[11] This is based on an examination question from the Chartered Institute of Management Accounting, also quoted in *Principles of Management*.

[12] In 360-degree feedback, a manager tells a staff member about their strengths and weaknesses in doing their job, and the staff member reciprocates by telling the manager about their strengths and weaknesses as a manager.

[13] It isn't a good idea to adopt the attitude of the mythical Irishman: "If I wanted to get there, I wouldn't start from here!"

Sources

For those wishing to explore how to improve specific aspects of management – for example, time management or motivational skills – there are a great many books readily available in bookshops and libraries. For those interested in the sources we used in writing this book, we found our quotations in a variety of places. When you are looking for them they crop up everywhere, like the win+win situation we saw in the film *The Beautiful Mind*.

Readers may be interested in searching for memorable phrases for each of our virtues in such books as:

God's Little Devotional Book for the Workplace, Todd Hafer, Eagle Publishing, Guildford (2001).

Grampas Are for All Seasons, Richard J. Ward, First Books Library, Bloomington, Indiana (2001).

Seize the Day: 366 tips for living, edited by Stephanie Weinrich and Nicholas Albery, Chatto & Windus, London (2001).

The Oxford Dictionary of Modern Quotations, Oxford University Press (2002).

The Oxford Dictionary of Quotations, Oxford University Press (2004).

The Ultimate Book of Business Quotations, Stuart Crainer, Capstone, Oxford (1997).

Appendix: Self-Assessment Forms

These forms will help you assess which of the virtues for managing you possess and which you don't. Each page addresses a single virtue, and is in two halves. The top half assesses the extent to which you are (a) a good manager or (b) a poor manager right now. The lower half is for repeating the exercise in, say, three months' time to assess how much progress you have made.

The left-hand side of the page lists some of the actions typical of good managers. Against each action, you should mark whether you do them always, usually, sometimes or never. Then do the same on the right-hand side of the page for the list of actions associated with poor managers.

When you have finished your assessment, review your response and draw your own conclusions about your overall level of performance. You should identify specific things you can do to improve your performance as a manager: for example, "Stop deluding yourself – be more self-critical."

At the end of the form, note down what you think your priorities should be for improving your use of the virtues for managing. As time goes by, keep going back to look at that page to help you focus on the actions you need to take to become a better manager.

INITIAL/FOLLOW-UP* ASSESSMENT OF YOUR PERFORMANCE
*Delete as applicable

Virtue 1:	Good managers have the courage to confront uncomfortable situations.

Mark what you do in the tables below!

GOOD Managers	Always	Usually	Sometimes	Seldom
Are willing to talk				
Put all their cards on the table				
Call a spade a spade				
Are self-critical				
Action plan to make you a Good Manager more often!				

POOR Managers	Always	Usually	Sometimes	Seldom
Run away from problems				
Address only symptoms				
Sweep things under the carpet				
Blame others				
Action plan to make you a Poor Manager less often!				

Date: _____

INITIAL/FOLLOW-UP* ASSESSMENT OF YOUR PERFORMANCE
*Delete as applicable

Virtue 2:	Good managers understand their priorities.

Mark what you do in the tables below!

GOOD Managers	Always	Usually	Sometimes	Seldom
Stop and think before acting				
Do first things first				
Always do the important things				
Are always busy but never too busy				
Action plan to make you a Good Manager more often!				

POOR Managers	Always	Usually	Sometimes	Seldom
Are very busy but don't achieve much				
Chop and change in their work				
Miss important deadlines				
Never say no to more work				
Action plan to make you a Poor Manager less often!				

Date: _____

INITIAL/FOLLOW-UP* ASSESSMENT OF YOUR PERFORMANCE

*Delete as applicable

Virtue 3:	Good managers know their objectives.

Mark what you do in the tables below!

GOOD Managers	Always	Usually	Sometimes	Seldom
Regularly clarify their objectives				
Write their objectives down				
Ask "What are we trying to do?"				
Use their objectives to measure progress.				
Action plan to make you a Good Manager more often!				

POOR Managers	Always	Usually	Sometimes	Seldom
Are vague about what they are trying to achieve				
Often change their objectives				
Find it difficult to make decisions				
Lack focus in their work and activities				
Action plan to make you a Poor Manager less often!				

Date: _____

INITIAL/FOLLOW-UP* ASSESSMENT OF YOUR PERFORMANCE
*Delete as applicable

Virtue 4:	Good managers listen and learn.

Mark what you do in the tables below!

GOOD Managers	Always	Usually	Sometimes	Seldom
Listen more than they talk				
Ask advice				
Look for feedback				
Explore ideas with people				
Action plan to make you a Good Manager more often!				

POOR Managers	Always	Usually	Sometimes	Seldom
Think they know the answer				
Are impulsive				
Have the "not invented here" syndrome				
Are cocksure				
Action plan to make you a Poor Manager less often!				

Date: _____

INITIAL/FOLLOW-UP* ASSESSMENT OF YOUR PERFORMANCE
*Delete as applicable

Virtue 5:	Good managers know themselves.

Mark what you do in the tables below!

GOOD Managers	Always	Usually	Sometimes	Seldom
Are realistic about their abilities				
Admit their shortcomings				
Are happy to delegate				
Ask for help from others				
Action plan to make you a Good Manager more often!				

POOR Managers	Always	Usually	Sometimes	Seldom
Will tackle everything				
Bite off more than they can chew				
Tend to be introspective				
Take risks on what they can do.				
Action plan to make you a Poor Manager less often!				

Date: _____

INITIAL/FOLLOW-UP* ASSESSMENT OF YOUR PERFORMANCE
*Delete as applicable

Virtue 6:	Good managers believe in teams.

Mark what you do in the tables below!

GOOD Managers	Always	Usually	Sometimes	Seldom
Share their problems				
Use the skills of their staff				
Accept the consensus view				
Invest time to know their staff				
Action plan to make you a Good Manager more often!				

POOR Managers	Always	Usually	Sometimes	Seldom
Keep things to himself				
Deal with staff individually, not as a team				
Rarely organise staff meetings				
Have weak relationships with staff				
Action plan to make you a Poor Manager less often!				

Date: _____

INITIAL/FOLLOW-UP* ASSESSMENT OF YOUR PERFORMANCE
*Delete as applicable

Virtue 7:	Good managers believe in delegation.

Mark what you do in the tables below!

GOOD Managers	Always	Usually	Sometimes	Seldom
Actively delegate				
Use the skills of their staff				
Always have their door open				
Action plan to make you a Good Manager more often!				

POOR Managers	Always	Usually	Sometimes	Seldom
Are a bottleneck				
Work excessively long hours				
Don't know the capabilities of their staff				
Action plan to make you a Poor Manager less often!				

Date: _____

INITIAL/FOLLOW-UP* ASSESSMENT OF YOUR PERFORMANCE
*Delete as applicable

Virtue 8:	Good managers know the value of time.

Mark what you do in the tables below!

GOOD Managers	Always	Usually	Sometimes	Seldom
Always have time to do their work				
Can find time to do extra key work				
Meet their deadlines				
Are open about allocating their time				
Action plan to make you a Good Manager more often!				

POOR Managers	Always	Usually	Sometimes	Seldom
Take shortcuts to meet deadlines				
Are late for appointments				
Spend time on unimportant things				
Leave things to the last moment				
Action plan to make you a Poor Manager less often!				

Date: _____

INITIAL/FOLLOW-UP* ASSESSMENT OF YOUR PERFORMANCE

*Delete as applicable

Virtue 9:	Good managers believe in people development.

Mark what you do in the tables below!

GOOD Managers	Always	Usually	Sometimes	Seldom
See every task as a chance to develop people				
Set stretching targets				
Help others to do things for themselves				
Action plan to make you a Good Manager more often!				

POOR Managers	Always	Usually	Sometimes	Seldom
Regard training as being for the training department				
Rob the training budget				
Think showing staff how to do things is a waste of time				
Action plan to make you a Poor Manager less often!				

Date: _____

INITIAL/FOLLOW-UP* ASSESSMENT OF YOUR PERFORMANCE
*Delete as applicable

Virtue 10:	Good managers are motivators.

Mark what you do in the tables below!

GOOD Managers	Always	Usually	Sometimes	Seldom
Praise or reprimand others fairly, using facts				
Distinguish effort from effect				
Look after his staff				
Action plan to make you a Good Manager more often!				

POOR Managers	Always	Usually	Sometimes	Seldom
Point out what is wrong and harp on it				
Praise their staff only occasionally				
Steal the ideas of their staff				
Action plan to make you a Poor Manager less often!				

Date: _____

INITIAL/FOLLOW-UP* ASSESSMENT OF YOUR PERFORMANCE
*Delete as applicable

Virtue 11:	Good managers are in control.

Mark what you do in the tables below!

GOOD Managers	Always	Usually	Sometimes	Seldom
Plan, monitor and follows through				
Don't panic				
Build feedback loops				
Think widely about what is possible				
Action plan to make you a Good Manager more often!				

POOR Managers	Always	Usually	Sometimes	Seldom
Have to cope with crises				
Worry over unlikely possibilities				
Tend to pass the buck				
Abdicate responsibility				
Action plan to make you a Poor Manager less often!				

Date: _____

INITIAL/FOLLOW-UP* ASSESSMENT OF YOUR PERFORMANCE
*Delete as applicable

Virtue 12:	Good managers look for win+win situations.

Mark what you do in the tables below!

GOOD Managers	Always	Usually	Sometimes	Seldom
Put themselves in others' shoes				
Don't regard their opponent as an enemy				
Visualise the impact on everyone				
Action plan to make you a Good Manager more often!				

POOR Managers	Always	Usually	Sometimes	Seldom
Have a "we win/you lose" attitude				
Accept short-term gains at the cost of long-term losses				
Usually fail in negotiations				
Action plan to make you a Poor Manager less often!				

Date: _____

INITIAL/FOLLOW-UP* ASSESSMENT OF YOUR PERFORMANCE

*Delete as applicable

Virtue 13:	Good managers take decisions and stick to them.

Mark what you do in the tables below!

GOOD Managers	Always	Usually	Sometimes	Seldom
Know not deciding carries a cost				
Aren't trigger happy				
Make decisions in good time				
Action plan to make you a Good Manager more often!				

POOR Managers	Always	Usually	Sometimes	Seldom
Never find time to complete the analysis				
Are afraid of being wrong				
Change their mind				
Action plan to make you a Poor Manager less often!				

Date: _____

INITIAL/FOLLOW-UP* ASSESSMENT OF YOUR PERFORMANCE
*Delete as applicable

Virtue 14:	Good managers are results oriented.

Mark what you do in the tables below!

GOOD Managers	Always	Usually	Sometimes	Seldom
Are focused on their targets				
Think ends and not means are key				
Follow through their decisions				
Action plan to make you a Good Manager more often!				

POOR Managers	Always	Usually	Sometimes	Seldom
Think in terms of doing things				
Don't reach conclusions for action				
Don't deliver on time				
Action plan to make you a Poor Manager less often!				

Date: _____

INITIAL/FOLLOW-UP* ASSESSMENT OF YOUR PERFORMANCE

*Delete as applicable

Virtue 15:	Good managers are imaginative.

Mark what you do in the tables below!

GOOD Managers	Always	Usually	Sometimes	Seldom
Asks: who? what? where? when? how? why?				
Think laterally				
Explore all possibilities				
Action plan to make you a Good Manager more often!				

POOR Managers	Always	Usually	Sometimes	Seldom
Accept the status quo				
Are scared of exploring				
Think in straight lines				
Conform to accepted thinking				
Action plan to make you a Poor Manager less often!				

Date: _____

PRIORITIES AFTER YOUR INITIAL SELF-ASSESSMENT

In the table below, mark the payoff you think you will obtain from achieving realistic improvements in your application of each virtue. You can then use the results to identify the priorities on which to focus so as to improve your overall performance as a manager.

Virtue for managing	The payoff from realistic improvement			
	Very significant	Significant	Some	Limited
1. Having courage to confront situations				
2. Understanding priorities				
3. Knowing objectives				
4. Listening and learning				
5. Knowing oneself				
6. Believing in teams				
7. Believing in delegation				
8. Knowing the value of time				
9. Believing in people development				
10. Being a motivator				
11. Being in control				
12. Looking for win+win outcomes				
13. Taking decisions and sticking with them				
14. Being results-oriented				
15. Being imaginative				
Using all the management virtues				

Your priorities:

PRIORITIES AFTER YOUR FOLLOW-UP SELF-ASSESSMENT

In the table below, mark the payoff you think you will obtain from achieving realistic improvements in your application of each virtue. You can then use the results to identify the priorities on which to focus so as to further improve your overall performance as a manager.

Virtue for managing	The payoff from realistic improvement			
	Very significant	Significant	Some	Limited
1. Having courage to confront situations				
2. Understanding priorities				
3. Knowing objectives				
4. Listening and learning				
5. Knowing oneself				
6. Believing in teams				
7. Believing in delegation				
8. Knowing the value of time				
9. Believing in people development				
10. Being a motivator				
11. Being in control				
12. Looking for win+win outcomes				
13. Taking decisions and sticking with them				
14. Being results-oriented				
15. Being imaginative				
Using all the management virtues				

Your priorities:

About the Authors

MICHAEL HOYLE has over thirty years' experience of advising managers and investors on organisational and business problems. His clients include leading international companies, banks, UK and foreign ministries, and international agencies. He is a Fellow of both the Chartered Management Institute and the Institute of Management Consultancy, and holds degrees from the University of London, the University of Chicago and the London School of Economics.

PETER NEWMAN has been a manager, a consultant and a teacher. Educated at McGill University and the Ivy Business School at the University of Western Ontario, he has taught business strategy, marketing, consumer behaviour and interpersonal skills to middle and senior managers as well as undergraduates at the University of Surrey. He has worked in the banking, retailing, manufacturing and transport sectors and gained experience that extends from shop-floor operations to management development and training.

The authors can be reached via *www.simplyagreatmanager.com*

Books in the Business Solutions Series

EFFECTIVE DECISION MAKING
10 steps to better decision making and problem solving |
Jeremy Kourdi

The very pressure for a decision often breeds indecisiveness This book enables you to find the best solutions and options, avoid pitfalls, manage risk, work with people to ensure that decisions succeed, and understand how you can improve the way you typically operate when making decisions.

BRILLIANT COMMUNICATION
5 steps to communicating your message clearly and effectively | Patrick Forsyth

Both written and presentational business communication are career skills in which one simply must excel. This book reviews the key factors that will help you prepare and communicate clearly, effectively and memorably.

THE NEW RULES OF ENTREPRENEURSHIP
What it really takes to become a savvy and successful entrepreneur | Rob Yeung

Combining genuinely practical advice with an easily digestible format, Rob Yeung guides you through the things you need to know in order to set up on your own business. This book shows you how to get motivated, make a business plan and sell your product quickly and effectively.

GREAT SELLING SKILLS
How to sell anything to anyone | Bob Etherington
Written in a quick-read and practical way, this book presents a set of simple, basic skills for selling, aimed exclusively at those people who have never been trained in the art of selling. Great Sellings Skills is intended to enable anyone to make a sound contribution to the overall sales process.

THE NEW RULES OF JOBHUNTING
A modern guide to finding the job you want | Rob Yeung
Job hunting is a job in itself. But too many books are aimed at helping career no-hopers get into a job – any job. This book is aimed at helping ambitious high fliers to, well, fly even higher. It will make sure you get the right job and maintain upward momentum in your career.

MANAGE YOUR BOSS
How to create the ideal working relationship | Patrick Forsyth
This book will enable you to create a relationship with your boss as something that can potentially help you do a good job and to meet specific job objectives. It also provides advice and tips on collaborating and working in parallel with your boss.

GREAT NEGOTIATING SKILLS
The essential guide to getting what you want | Bob Etherington
This book is packed with anecdotes and advice for all those people who are generally terrible at negotiating and would like to do it better.

SURVIVING OFFICE POLITICS
Coping and succeeding in the workplace jungle | Patrick Forsyth

Office politics happens – whether you want to admit it or not. But politicking need not always be bad. Here is the definitive answer to engaging with office politics to further your own career in a positive fashion– and deal with the Machiavellian types and pre-empt their efforts.

ESSENTIAL TIME MANAGEMENT
How to become more productive and effective | Brett Hilder

Using your time effectively can transform your personal productivity and determine your level of success. This book provides a practical framework to help anyone manage their time better at work, inspiring certain mental attitudes and thinking towards the working day and the tasks facing you.

SIMPLY A GREAT MANAGER
The fundamentals of being a successful manager | Mike Hoyle & Peter Newman

Like many things in life, becoming a great manager is in fact a simple process – if only we knew how and changed our current habits. The authors in this book have identified 15 fundamental principles that can easily be followed by mere mortals when they have something or somebody to manage.